How to Tattoo

& Start-Up Business

By Hitachi Choparazzi

Acknowledgements

To all the inspiring tattooists/artists that want to start a career in tattoos that cannot get into a shop apprenticeship, or that cannot get sponsored to begin starting to tatt, and there is no trade school for tattoos currently to teach people, nor programs of apprenticeships for tatting. I want to take the time to acknowledge your fire & desire to be a tatt artist!

ATTN:

This *How to Tattoo* book is a Tattoo 101 fundamentals book. This is a guideline meant to follow and help you learn how to tattoo thru textbook framework, tips, and preventative solutions. Also, an Audible way to learn how to tattoo.

However, this is not a tattoo visual book. You still need hands-on experience to develop and practice how to tattoo also. This book is only intended to give you the proper education and learn how and what to do before you actually start your hands-on experience in tattooing. This book is meant to help prepare you, educate you, and give you the correct confidence boost you need to tattoo and tackle any piece.

This book is not guaranteed to make you an instant tattoo artist and inkmaster or instant gratification and the best results sought merely from just reading it. It is solely up to you to put in the work, time, practice, and apply yourself to be the best tattoo artist and business owner as possible. A true skillset is developed.

Foreword

I took the time out to handwrite this *How to Tattoo and Start-Up* book for all of you seekers and youth that want to truly chase your dreams and passion for art and tattoos. Art and tattoos are synonyms, and tattooing is a rare but ancient art form. It's been around since the ancient tribal times despite how some people in society will say it's still taboo and not a real profession in the new digital era of natives and consumers.

There is no tattoo trade school or a lot of apprenticeship programs for most beginners to start at. Most people are self-taught and just learn through trial and error of experience with others such as friends and family members in a garage. Therefore, they don't have a guideline or true help and someone that is a professional or expert tattoo artist to consult or ask the questions they need answers to and tips or pointers, quality and strategies.

I decided to add value to impact each of all the new inspiring tattoo artists up and coming with a passion to help carve out a clear path of success from my experience as an expert artist of 16-plus years and shop owner. To be able to help by talking to thousands of inspiring artists all at once while providing true professional aspects, tips, and solid regimen to abide by. I hope all you guests appreciate, learn, and use this book as your tattoo 101 and start-up blueprint to start on a successful career of longevity and reaching your passion and fulfilments. Enjoy this read or Audible and let's begin a new chapter of your life with the first chapter of this how-to book. I believe in you all if nobody else don't, and know the start-up strong hustle, and power of confidence it takes. Plus your reputation on the line to trust your gut, by following your passion, while attempting to hush silence your fears of messing up or tackling each different tattoo project. Let's fix all that and the butterflies. Let's go!

Contents

- Chapter 1 -

"Tattoo 101"

The art of tattooing and the rare art form of tattooing with traditional tattoo machines or ancient tapping utensils. All have the love of art with the intentions to be the ultimate ink master at your culture and skillset craft. Tattoo is defined as an indelible figure fixed upon the body especially by insertion of pigment under the skin. Pigmentation is coloration with or deposition of pigment, especially an excessive deposition of body pigment. The dermal 7 layer of skin, and dermis is the aim of how deep you want to go with your needles. However, be careful not too deep to puncture the dermis, which is the sensitive vascular inner layer of skin. We will get into all of this further into the book, also.

The objective and main focal point is for you to learn all the fundamentals how to tattoo. This book is for you to gain all the knowledge and basics of tattooing 101 before you gain actually hands-on experience to prevent you from mistakes, scarring people, or spreading bloodborne diseases. Remember tattoos are permanent and to be taken serious, safe practices along with cleaning and disinfecting. These effective methods, principles, tips, and tools will really enable you how to tattoo and start-up your own tattoo business successfully. I've decided to help you solve all your tattoo how-to start-up problems, and answer all the questions you have, or would run into without having nobody to steer you correct and back on your tattoo path. All this without fear! You can learn a lot by reading, visual, and Audible especially how to tattoo correctly if you pay attention, study, and observe how to tackle any tattoo head-on with artistry and confidence. Most of all developing your own signature style of tattoo with a steady and flaming hot hand that everyone is talking about and buzzing with positive reviews of your work and influence around the shop, city, and social media, in a global all-around showcase of some of your best masterpieces you tackled. Now let's start you into tattoo 101 now that you open and content with confidence. This book will give you the courage, skillset, and competitive edge you need to be a dominant tattoo artist and shop owner.

First, you need to be able to sketch or draw. Even taking sketch classes or practicing at home by your own. Surprisingly a fun fact is that a lot of tattoo artists cannot draw very well or too much at all. However, they can sketch and trace immaculate. They can do the layout automated thru digital pro tools like MacBook, art windows, and stencil templates with digital sketch pens. Also, there are plenty of tutorials, webinars on artist drawing, or sketching on their digital devices and tools to format anything you want to sketch and draw. These can be viewed with your mobile device anywhere or time you ready to learn and get started.

Sketching and drawing is just like any other thing you set out to do in life, with practical aim and focus you accomplish what you seek. Especially if you work at perfecting your craft daily like Kobe Bryant you'll master it. Remember, becoming a signature style inkmaster is the ultimate goal. Therefore, you should have that into your mindset that you will be great and can tackle anything you have in front of you long as you put in the intense work behavior and ethic it takes. Same as acquiring any skillset.

If tattoos are your passion, then you should treat taking the initial next step to take time out and perfect your drawing craft. It should be treated as a passion project. Despite even if you already started drawing on your own or already developed your style of drawing, you should still be open to other ways to gain the experience and not to get stuck or blindsided on a piece you cannot draw that the customer wants. You can always learn more from others and never have too much practice. Transparency and transition.

Now once you have caught on to how to sketch and draw with a steady hand, next you need to start off by tracing. Trace all your patterns on drawing paper, stencils, or e-devices. I prefer the old-school way of paper or rice paper if you at home, to reverse the paper or stencil to trace over the whole pattern. Doing this time and time again is great practice to help keep your hand in motion, rhythm, and to develop a steady hand of staying in line. Once you pick up on tracing patterns it comes natural your hand and alignment. I highly suggest this because you cannot practice runs on people, and afford to make a swivel line sabotaging the client's tattoo and risk not getting paid for your services, and a bad reputation and name for doing bad work, and blotching people's tatts. The main objective is for you to get the stroke and flow of it down before you tattoo. For years before I would start to do a client tattoo, I'd trace over the pattern on the stencils before I laid it down to tackle the tattoo. This format enabled me to know how I wanted to do the tattoo; which angles were easier versus complex. Also the starting points and which lines were to hit before I'd back myself into a corner where you cannot go up or around because the stencil wore off from wiping and I had to freestyle the lines no longer visible. So my tracing the pattern beforehand habit that I built became automatic. I did not panic, instead I pushed thru it with no anxiety in my craft. Remember, create practices systematic until it becomes automatic process. A prime example of this is using the keypad. Let's say you cannot remember a phone number or a password you use regularly. However, if you look at that dial or keypad and use your hand, it automatically presses in the code or punches in those same numbers because you developed a system that became an automatic habit of practice where it's natural to the body, senses, and systematic.

Starting the actual tattoo on someone, first you want to lay out the stencil correctly by centering it and making sure it's not placed reversed or backwards when it's the other way around or misspelled words, etc....always confide with your client to show them for approval and double-check, never assume how they would like it, want it, or need it. Remember tattoos are forever. Also your reputation is priceless and grows the base of your business and clientele. Allow your clients to look at the tattoo beforehand in the mirror first before you start their tatt.

Next is how to set-up and adjust your machine and gun. You can go online or to your local tattoo art supplies shops to buy start tattoo kits including gun, gloves, multiple gauge needles, several different colors of ink. Each machine should have a foot pedal to control the throttle of the gun. To set-up your gun you'll need to adjust the back of it and twist the knob until it's a slight gap, no more than the size of a dime for it to come on. However, if you adjust your gun with more of the back knob to gap a nickel size, it will not work or cut on, no matter how much you hit the foot pedal. It should be the width equivalent of a dime, not the width of a nickel. You can adjust your machine speed for settings like if you need to slow it down to shade or speed it up to hit your line work more effective and one-take Jake.

Now setting your needles in place is essential. You must be able to always see your needle point and head as your guide or else you're risking your tattoo and messing up completely out of pattern. Even if there is a bunch of ink spots that all suddenly splat over your lines stencils pattern, you need to stop, wipe, and also wipe your gun off. No need to panic. It's usually from you dipping your gun into the ink for longer durations. You should only have a one-one thousand, two-one thousand count, that's all. When you pour your ink into the cap you are dipping out of to tattoo, you can put Vaseline at the bottom of the cap to help the ink stick better. It's not required, but a highly practice most artists use effectively.

The needles can be 3 gauges, 5 gauges, 7 gauges, it all depends on if you are tackling a piece with a lot of shading, you'll want to use more needles. Single needles is still used but not commonly singular used. Typically you would start out using one single needle until you build confidence to use more gauge needles. I personally would use 3 gauge needles for my lines and hard line works or detail-intense lines. Then typical shading will range from 5 to 7 needles running out my gun. The typical tattoo time is an hour and a half for basic tattoos. Therefore, you have to be committed, highly focused, and able to see your needle sticking out no more than a quarter of an inch. If it's poked out too far, it could snag the skin or bounce off line. Or if your adjustments to your machine is too slow, it may also snag the skin and bounce around off line. Also if your needle is barely poking out of the gun, you can barely see what lines you are tatting. This will cause you to only see the ink flow, and not the needle flowing to guide your path of tattoo.

The rubber band keeps the needle steady and in place wrapped around the needle and back of the gun. It also helps the machine noise vibrations down a notch. Most clients do get intimidated by the loud drilling buzz sound of the tattoo machine. Remember your job is to make them feel safe, sound, and create a great environment, providing a comfortable experience.

You need to always hold the gun firmly and get your gripping down with confidence. How you hold the tattoo gun dictates the tattoo outcome and hiccups or inconsistency. The proper way is to rest the back of the gun in between the web of your thumb and index finger to take the weight of the machine off most of the tattoo time. However, you do not have to use this practice. Most of the time you tatt you'll be holding your gun upright. People all tattoo different from their gripping, to sideways angles you name. It's all your preference and your own signature style that you develop with comfort and skillset for the best quality tatts for your customers. Not all tattoo guns models are the same, especially with custom-built machines that's straight up and down and ultra lightweight.

To practice on alternate canvas like pig skin, synthetic skin, styro cups, even orange peel skins, I've seen it all. It's good to practice your line work and steady hand before you try an actual human canvas. It's also different skins, different styles, different skin type canvas. You have bleeders, thin skin, sensitive skin, rough skin, darker skin, also scarring easy, and rejecting ink, too. Additional to hard placement tattoos and canvas like armpits, and ribs, or even tackling a back piece. Tattooing on bones is more of a challenge area too. Therefore, you need to be aware and understand all of this and these troubleshoot areas beforehand starting.

Tattoos is each challenges if you like challenges and passionate. Have your game plan down how to tackle the tatt and not going too deep to scar people. Confidence you got be 100 percent every time you pick up that machine to go to work. Tatting good line work and consistency is key.

Tatting is becoming more popular globally and accepted more nowadays. From TV shows, reality shows and challenges to the NBA players doing face tatts, which also became the new norm versus taboo just 10 years ago. You also have judges, lawyers, and lawmakers nowadays all sleeved down with tattoos. All a global phenomenon and a promising career trade to practice and step into a sure community. Usually apprenticeships going into shops to clean up, help out, and learn from artists their tools, craft, and tricks to develop and transition for starters.

However, you can begin with yourself without a tattoo shop sponsor or apprenticeship program. You just need to own that you are the artist and is empowerment to overcome challenges or understanding challenges. You must know who you are to embrace and overcome all challenges and obstacles as a tattoo artist. The ribs is a thinner layer of skin to tatt and also a harder area. You cannot refuse to do it, or suck your teeth and convince your clients to pick another easier area to tatt. Instead you must overcome all fear and have confidence. Remember the more practice, the better the experience you developed and artist you will become. Practice makes good aim and you to become perfect by mastery.

It is important daily to always remember your focal points of why you tattoo, and why people get tattoos. Tattooing is therapy and getting tattoos, too. Also release certain endorphins in the brain, pain and pleasure chemical release that some people like and prefer to de-stress. It's also wearing meaningful stories on your personal canvas. Each piece is meaningful and have significance, a symbol or time stamped, dated, or a memory of a loved one. To some it's being emotionally scarred literally. Either way it all seeks true purpose and has real meaning. Therefore, it's your job as the artist and expert to give them a great experience to feel comfortable and come back with great work and visuals they wanted.

The outline of your tattoo is the first thing you do to tackle your tattoo. Shading to solid is usually the last thing you do to finish. Figure out a focal point of your tattoo or drawing. Soft edges and values, soft lines versus hard lines. Dark b.g. (background) helps pop out your tattoo and light areas, too.

You can start off only doing names, letters, and numbers to get comfortable and more confidence to tackle bigger pieces and portraits. Start small at first, small lines and circles. Make consistent strokes in your lines. Do not lift your hand off a line mid-stroke while tatting. Have a starting A-to-B point, that you finish the ending line point before starting over to repeat the same process. It will become natural habit automated with more built confidence and practice. Again, this is another reason it's a good habit to build when you practice trace your stencil pattern beforehand as previously described. Remember, this is a key tool they don't teach you, or tell you about during your tattoo apprenticeship program. However, you usually discover only thru experience and being self-taught after running into a few line hiccups and shaky non-consistency. If your hard lines are off, they offset the whole tattoo. Remember, the sole purpose is to save you time, costly errors, and your reputation. Therefore, your line work is very essential for all great tatts.

When doing your first line work you must again make sure you can see your needle tatting the skin. You must not go too deep to scar a person's skin, instead going too light press, it won't stick the ink. You must break the dermis at a medium press. You can see and follow your outline of the ink into the skin, then evaluate if the skin is absorbing the ink correctly. You can do a simple wipe-off or down of your tattoo first lines as a test. It will show if the ink is sticking correctly or rejecting it. What you want to look for correctly after you do a progress or security wipe of the line work is for it to be embedded into the skin all the way and consistently without spots, dark/light or skipped spaces. It will also be dark and by eyeballing it after you already wiped, it should reveal the exact permanent mark you need to sustain the completion of the tattoo. This is a huge hang-up and misguided method that people cannot grasp off tops and their first actually test client they scar going too deep or they go too light and the tattoo scabs quickly and all the ink falls out, which kills all effort and confidence morale. Of course with practices and determination you'll eventually catch on. However, by this major tip of teaching you how to correctly press the needle into the skin to avoid these rookie mistakes and your reputation, save you time, money, and effort. You must find a medium press rhythm and stroke that you develop and get down pat. It's very essential if you want to declare yourself as an inkmaster and a long career of the art of tattooing.

Now that we are on the subject of wipe-downs, I'll show you the process. You get your sterile rag or cloth and damp it a little bit. Not too wet or too dry. The basis for this is to wipe any extra ink off outside the tattoo line work or stencil. This method enables you and act as an eraser to clear your path of the tattoo and monitor your progress. However, it's totally up to you how often you wipe off the tattoo. Some artists very little and rarely not at all until the end. I recommend from my 17 years of personal experience to wipe off every time after you hit a line or shade. Basically every time you pick your tatt gun off the skin, wipe and proceed again. I must not fail to mention some artists do not actually damp or wet their essential wipe cloths or rags, they just simply leave it dry. You have to be considerate of your clients and their agony. Getting a tattoo is already highly tense and actually painful to others. Therefore, a dry wipe cloth makes a rough wipe and uncomfortable for them. However, with a damped wipe cloth it's more soothing and smooth. It's all up to your discretion. I do highly recommend running an ethical practice.

Next, we will get into the act of how to shade and shading methods. Remember, on stretching the skin with your index finger and thumb opposite of your hand you are tatting with, not to overstretch the skin while shading or doing your line work. A nice stretch will do, just don't attempt to pull their skin too far apart.

When shading it's best to do with multiple gauge needles, 5, 7, or 9 needles. It helps to cover more area. You want to start your shading in doing circular shading motions. Small circles is for darker shading and bigger circles is for lighter shading. You can also adjust your machine speed and slow it down to help you shade better and more effectively. When you run your tatt machine higher, it's more better speed for outlines and line work. You have different ways to shade and styles like pepper shading and reverse shading. Make sure your shading is very consistent, too. No light spots or missed spots. Also, make sure shading does not overshadow your hard lines or go outside your lines.

Pepper shading is a light style of shading that gives it a pepper-looking effect. It looks if you sprayed pepper on the skin. It's also tip shading where it's more of an intimate close detail shading in intense proximately fine areas. Some artists prefer tip shading. Then it's reverse shading or better known as negative shading technique. Reverse shading is where you use the background to be the main canvas to pop out or the silhouette. You wouldn't have hard lines on the outside of your tattoo if you are reverse shading a piece on a client. Reverse shading is simply to show against a light background. And a silhouette is a representation of the outlines of an object filled in with black or some other uniform color. Example giving, think of the NY Yankees logo, especially on their ballcaps. Now imagine that on your canvas and you shade in all around the NY letters logo, leaving it blank to pop-out with no hard outlines. Of course you would do some traditional pepper shading or fading your transition from light to dark blend. This helps it going from light to heavy dark, which can look like a hard line or barrier and not a natural fade transition, especially if it's color, not just black and white, traditional.

Be careful with your transitions from dark to light, especially with shading and color. Color inside clean outlines, outlines have to be best and clean.

Shading dark to fade to light, start practicing shapes darker to light transitions. All the natural light spots leave light. If you're shading it in lightly, make sure the darker you shade the dark spots, too.

Next you need to know the challenging duties and difference playing with the colors and mixing and matching the ink colors. Color coordinator blends and mix with transitional. Color theory is making sure all the colors goes together and stand out. One wrong color offsets a tattoo and makes it horrible or a terrible irreversible mistake. Color palette is a compound of coloring/colors.

Remember, slowing down the machine for adjustments to do dots, not too slow to snag skin blowouts. Bold outlines, hit nice details clean, solid outline, shaded. Nice black and grey, color not too rich, stippling around it, open skin. Every part of the tatt have to be clear what it is. Not too much craziness, some things are light shading as a minor little touch. Your color blend can't be off.

Now we will tackle subject and content style. Adaptability on style and subject with all and every new tatt. Like American traditional and like doing a tiger head. Or a neo-traditional tatt. There are several different styles of tattoos and subjects can vary but are mainly theme based or personal storylines. Some examples of the main styles you'll be tatting daily at the shop for people choices are black and grey, color, simply, wild, and also concoctions of style. For instance a concoction style of traditional, animate, and black and grey. From lettering, American traditional (color), and illustrative. Remember it's very important that when using letters, your opening letter has to stick out, no cluttering words, and must be legible. Also to remember your consistency on line is key, no waver moments. How to deal with your canvas style and subject, do not sculpter lines on top of lines. Do not undershade in areas, use a cool stroke motion, no shaky outlines and wavery color.

You can Google different artwork style all over the 7 continents, including ancient styles. Then practice them and study them to get familiar and develop fundamental bases. This would most definitely help you if you get a client from overseas or with a tattoo pattern request from ancient styles of art. You'll be prepared. The best tattoo inkmasters are the ones who do not turn down clients and can tackle any tattoos, even the intense peculiar ones. You also are establishing a trust and bond relationship with your client to do the right job and your best professional work. They are trusting you to tattoo them like an expert versus a drunken tattoo artist. Again, keep in mind your rep is on the line and everything in this field of tattoo artistry. There is even a such thing as traditional hand poke tattoo techniques and string tattoo techniques and practices within tribal cultures and passed down ancient traditions. Both do not require an actual tattoo machine and gun. They also have their own methods and concoctions to make homemade ink. Tattoos methods are optional and have a long ancient history globally in all fashions. It's up to you on what type of tattoo method and style you want to take on to tatt your clients. However, the most commonly popular way to tattoo is by modern gun/machine and foot pedal. Even though some artists still prefer homemade tatt gun.

It is very important you have the proper lighting in the room, shop, or place you tattoo at. Most shops have the proper lighting. You can get lamps or light rings online like Amazon or eBay with high-quality light and watts. Lights is essential to see more vividly and enhance your sight to hit all your tattoo and small intense lines. Tattoos is about the best details. It's a good practice to have your additional lighting as a lamp or light ring, even if you have enough light in the room you tattoo in to see already. Having the full extra lighting on top of the tattoo is very essential and will always assist and enable you to do the best possible outcome. Every real inkmaster have established the proper lighting to work under rule of thumb.

Lastly let's go over this chapter with an overview rewind and a checklist of all the essential methods of How to Tattoo 101.

First off we will start with the courage and this first chapter giving you that extra boost of confidence to get started tattooing and the courage to tackle any piece on any canvas, including the harder, more thinner on bones areas of the canvas.

Then you must take the time out to properly learn how to sketch and freestyle drawing. Take a class and work on your skillset, including a bunch of tracing, lining, and shading with pen, pencil, and color pencils, too. Even practice drawing with your tablets and MacBook Pro sketch pads and e-pens. You can look for much art tutorials online to give you fundamentals and you can get your art degree and go to art school if you wish to take it that far, too.

You must remember everyone, including yourself, has the ability to draw anything—letters, shapes, etc. How you see it, break down to the simplest to do drawn. You can draw with time it takes, the practice, and a lot of desire.

Next is the pulling of the skin to tatt. Do not super stretch the skin when tattooing. It's okay to spread the skin as much as needed without overdoing it. Now remember when inking your canvas for the ink to stick correctly, you don't go too deep to scar a client. Nor too light for the ink not to stick and fall out like a scab of ink. You must find a medium press and a medium stroke tatting. You cannot go too fast, or too slow.

Then make sure you can see your needle at all times and wipe accordingly. Adjust your machine accordingly and make sure to gap it with the right dime width gap to get the right friction and current to power your machine in sync with foot pedal and adjustable knobs. Put a rubber around the frame and needle to help needle control and silence the machine down a notch. Remember the tattoo gun noise is very intimidating, especially for a first-timer getting tatted.

The main theme for tatting is quality and consistency. No spotted or half shading. Your shading has to be spot-on and all your colors coordinated, also your color transition impeccable. Small circles at a time shading smaller areas and to get it darker in depth. You can also use multiple needles and slow your tatt machine down to the adjustable speed you need.

Outlines and all lines have to also be consistent and very crisp clean. Not rushed or rough to get away from you. Bang out the most of the tattoo without no hiccups or wobbles in your hard lines, or lines period. Remember it is key you need solid lines, and clean body of work, and consistency.

The tattoo community and at expos have a Friday the 13th tattoo marathon tradition which a lot of shops participate in, which is where we tattoo for 13 hours straight from 5 different flash challenges designs for people. Like quick banger tatts, some outlines other traditional, or whatever style you can manage and prefer. Again, to do this you need to be able to have quality and consistency.

Finally remember don't be impulsive in a rush to get in there to attempt to tattoo and mess someone up, or pass a bloodborne disease without proper sanitation practices and the correct competence to tattoo your canvas and how it all works. Whereas, your rep is everything, especially in the beginning.

- Chapter 2 -

"Sanitation, Safety, & Hazards"

In this chapter we will be going over the sanitation, safety practice, and hazards in the work environment. Proper preparation on sanitation to tattoo and the workspace for you and your clients' health and safety is very essential. From dealing with needles, bloody wipe rags, to wrapping your tattoos afterwards properly. You risk infection and infecting others, too.

Thru bloodborne diseases, pathogens, and using unsterile materials and utensils, you can spread hepatitis, possibly HIV, MRSA, and so much more. A healthy mind is essential for a powerful tattoo. However, a health practice is best and important for all tattoo artists' and clients' well-being. The health and welfare of your shop, booth, chair, or garage. Wherever you tattoo, that environment needs to be sterile, safe, and clean practices. It shouldn't curate germs, old bloody rags, or a breeding ground for bacteria or bloodborne diseases, period.

Bloodborne means airborne. Therefore when you tatting in any form or body piercing, you are actually penetrating the skin and run risk off top for bloodborne disease and infections. That smell of blood when you enter a tattoo shop or getting a tatt you smell a familiar copper smell. Some people say it smells like pennies. However, that smell of blood, just as it clings on to your nose hairs, is sure as pathogens can cling to the tiny fiber hair of your lungs and respiratory system.

Pathogens is a specific agent as bacterium causing disease. Also blood poisoning is highly possible too with a bad practice of sterilization and proper disinfectants. Blood poisoning is an invasion of bloodstream by microbes from infection. Whereas, an infection is a disease or condition caused by a germ or parasite. Therefore, as an active tattoo artist you need to beware of all these diseases bloodborne and terminologies to protect your clients, yourself, and your business or work environments. Proper precautions comes with the know-how to keep your clients and work environments safe and sanitized justly, and with the proper protective gear like plastic latex gloves and mask. Even glasses is taken as a preventive safety measure, but not mandatory. It's totally up to the artist if they choose to wear glasses or protective safety goggles so no droplets or anything goes directly into your eyes or blur your vision. You cannot tattoo without focusing and you need great visuals to accomplish that, too.

Now let's get into sanitation and good practices of sterilization at your shop, workstation, and total equipment. The word sterilization is being free from germs and to make sterile. You can use sterilizer like sprays and chemicals to disinfect tattoo guns, machines, utensils, chairs, and workstations. Alcohol pads and Clorox wipes, too.

First the number 1 rule with safety and sanitation is to never use the same needles twice, or the same materials like such as gloves and wipe cloths, etc. Always use new presterilized needle for each new tattoo and client. Do not save certain needles for certain client to save cost. Please, do not put nobody's health or life in jeopardy, or risk losing your shop or tattoo permits and license. It's not worth it and all tattoo paraphernalia is inexpensive. You can buy in bundles online or in bulk at your local tattoo supplies chain stores in your city. Don't risk infection cutting corners.

You can also buy all biodegradable materials that you can throw away after one use, it's inexpensive, too. I prefer to use biodegradable and eco-friendly materials, too. All of these can be found online, too, from biodegradable gloves to wipes. Take the time out to do your Google searches correctly. A side note and quick bonus tip on SEO is to do your searches and URLs for niche items or specialization in quotes for direct best search results. For instance Google search How to Tattoo, see the results. Then Google search in quotes "How to Tattoo" and notice all the direct focus and difference. The increase can improve all your direct niche items you're generating. Search presterilized tattoo needles in bulk for your best deals inexpensive of your choice or wholesale deals. Especially if you have a business tax license and registered merchant to get better bulk wholesale deals and prices.

The next major thing to know what not to do when dealing with needles is to make sure you get the right needles to tattoo with. Especially if you just starting out as a beginner artist at your trial stages. Do not make the mistake and buy the wrong needles. Mainly if you using homemade tattoo guns, utensils, or traditional hand poke tattoo techniques. Particularly no hypodermic needles. Yes, I said no hypodermic needles. You would be surprised how so many people rush in without due knowledge to tatt off impulse, or just to make some quick cash. A hypodermic needle has a hollow hole for injecting material into or through the skin. It's the same exact needle used in a syringe except they are the small single hypodermic needles, people are attempting to tatt with. When you use these hypodermic needles you are risking injecting ink into someone direct bloodstream and body, not just their skin and dermal layers. Another mention, just FYI, not all needles you buy at tattoo supply stores or online goes for every single tattoo gun in the marketplaces. It's different makes and models, especially dealing with custom-made models or foreign-made machines with different metric system than the U.S. Again, make sure you do your research thoroughly before you get started A-thru-Z.

You can also go online and watch safety and sanitation courses how to sterilize and disinfect properly. The CDC (Centers for Disease Control and Prevention) website have all the COVID-19 disinfective chemical elements and solutions to use to sterilize your shop, workstation, and tattoo environments. They all vary and including the equipment used to disinfect and sterilize effectively. The CDC guidelines is updated regularly. It will also provide you with additional bloodborne disease and pathogens from tattooing.

There is in addition to safety and sanitation matters classes or courses you can actually take, not just watch online or Audible, which you can get certified. Like OSHA certified for safety and health administration. OSHA is abbreviated for Occupational Safety and Health Administration. However, you do not have to be OSHA certified to tattoo. It is just an example of various safety and health certification out there. Whereas, some cities, states, and counties may require you take a certain safety, health course, hours, and get certified before you can tattoo, get your permit, business license or tattoo license.

Next we will get into sanitation and safety of how to wrap, clean, and take care of your tattoo. This is retroactive to all the tatt artists and clients. Whereas, each tattoo artist can and should advise and instruct their clients all how to take care of their tattoo afterwards. Especially to risk infections, ink falling out, and best results. It's a great practice and excellent customer service skill. It shouldn't matter if your client canvas is tatted up from head-to-toe or a regular, it's still your job and duty to tell them proper instructions how to take care of their tattoo and heal properly and responsibly. I always warn my clients that it will itch like hell at some times and tattoos during heal stages of new skin coat process. Then please do not risk scratching it with your nails being dirty and irritate it more and possibly get infected.

After you the artist is done doing your tattoo, you should clean it properly with the wipe cloth and water or soap and water. Make sure to get all the extra ink smudges from smearing ink wiping the tattoo off the skin before you wrap it up. After the tattoo is all clean and wiped down, apply Vaseline with a nice thick coat over the tattoo. Not too thin or too thick in a globber. This helps to keep the ink in the skin for the first 24 hours. Especially for the colors in the tattoo. Next you take plastic Saran Wrap to place over the tattoo and Vaseline, to keep the tattoo sealed in Vaseline in place. Last step is to tape the tattoo piece on your canvas for a finish final touch with preferably medical cloth tape that stick to the skin easy.

Then next thing to do is instruct your clients how to take care of their new tattoo work at home. Tell them after 24 hours it's okay to take the wrap off their tattoo or they can leave it on for longer, but to be careful not to smother it too much or too long. They can wash it regularly or when they get into the shower. Regular soap and water is fine. Remember not to apply too many additional incentives. Neosporin or lotion is fine. It's best to let your tattoo heal naturally. You can let the air hit it but be careful being in the sun or doing sweaty activity to push the ink out. The sun will making your ink fall out or fade and damage your tattoo with too much sun exposure. If they let their tattoo dry out too early, it can develop a hard scab which can end up in a scar on your tattoo pulling out a patch of ink, too. The ideal time is 72 hours you want to keep your tattoo moist. Some tattoos within 48 hours be done thru that healing process stage and dry out with little or no scabbing. Not all skin and tattoo areas on your canvas is the same and all heal different. It's different strokes for different folks. However, it's your responsibility to tell them how to take action and proper tattoo safety and sanitation implementation practices. They must not over-medicate and simply let their body skin heal naturally without no rush quick hacks. Don't pick at your tattoos, either. Remember, tattooing and getting tattoos is a de-stress and therapeutic to most. However, don't stress your skin and tattoo out afterwards. You must protect it by all means and keep it clean. Hands off is the best policy to prevent infections.

Making sure your values, your shop values, and customer values is all in regards to safety and sanitation practices. Post pandemic of COVID-19 even with all these different trial cures, you should still practice health and safety. You can still wear mask tatting and offer your clients N95 mask at your shop or workstations. PPE (personal protective equipment) is always essential in sanitation and safety, also a great outline and policy to practice. Again, it's not mandatory but bestow great tatting ethics and make your clients feel safe and comfortable, establishing a great experience and clientele to come back.

Lastly to finish this chapter we will address hazards. Yes, there are hazards in tatting additional to the tattoo environments, too. Precautions is not just for you and your customer, it's for your employees, guests and everyone entering in your establishment of tattooing.

In the business of tattooing comes with hazards of exposure because you are dealing with blood, needles, and multiple people daily. Anyone tattooing in an open space or garage, they need to be aware of the hazardous material. Keep all used needles, blood materials, and wipe rags in red biohazard bags separate from each one and regular non-hazardous trash. You can even use those yellow biohazard bags, too. Keep a separate portable trash can with a concealed lid at all times. The portable white or black trash cans need to be a separate color different from the rest of your trash cans in the shop or around the place you're tatting. This is to ensure people cleaning the shop and trash cans not to entangle both trash cans and someone get poked by a bloody used needle. Including once they dump the shop trash into the big dumpster out back. This is why the red biohazardous bags are recommended and highly used just like hospitals. It's usually someone specific trained to dispose the biohazard material correct. It's optional you can also have a place come pick-up these biohazardous material from the shop or place of tatting. However, just please to remember not to throw your red biohazard bags into the regular trash cans, risking someone getting exposed or losing your tattoo privilege and getting fined, then establishment shut down by the health inspector and department. Keep in mind that customers and employees can both sue you for negligence in a civil suit matter. It's also your job of identifying all the hazards that poses a threat to your staff or apprentice and interims in all workstations, areas, and with the machines, needles, electric, and chemicals. Hazards is anything that can present imminent danger or harm.

Get into great hazardous-free habits daily till you build reputation into normal practices. By identifying hazards like blood stained on your tattoo table, bed, or chair. Even lodged into your tattoo machine. Droplets on the floor or hidden bloody used wipe cloths on the floor hidden out of sight. You need to be agile and very vigilant of identifying these precaution hazards, with interventions of being proactive and proper preparations.

These are a few preventative proper preparations for precautious tips. First clean all machines, stations, chairs, tables that you tattoo on, with, or at. By disinfecting with proper chemicals or Clorox wipes, wipe them down. Afterwards the secret I used is to wrap all my tatting sitting or laying consoles with sheet wrap or plastic. I also use these techniques with all my tattoo station equipment. For instance my cord, machine, etc., is all prewrapped with plastic, not to expose hazard matters or material. Then afterwards I exchange sheet wrap or plastic machine covers, etc., with each new individual I tattoo. You too should use this same implementation practice as a guideline and to set your shop and artist standards. These sheet wraps and plastic machine and table wraps can be found online and biograde disposable grade wraps. You can get them also in bulk and usually wholesale at your local tattoo supplies, too.

Remember always to sanitize your tattoo station and machine first before and after every single tattoo, no matter how little work or quick tattoo job you pull. Your position is always to run a safe and hazard-free environment with provided sanitation for all services you provide.

Finally, this is another important key hazard what not to do. Please, do not ever reuse the same ink on different people, or save it for the same client for another session and next day. Also do not use ink and the rest you have left pour it back into the ink bottle you originally pour it from. Please, do not try to cut corners by not wanting to waste ink. You run the risk of infecting people with diseases, virus, and pathogens. I had to stop someone from putting used ink back into a bottle to save on a certain unique color. You must be realistic and humane hazard-free optimistic 25/8.

- Chapter 3 -

"Developing Your Style"

Developing your style is your signature mark or stamp you are renowned for. Each artist should have a unique form of style that they can articulate and bring to life. Developing a tattoo signature style of tatting is what helps set your foundation for branding yourself for a household name. Owning that style and domain space of specialization as an inkmaster that only people will go to book a session with you for your exclusiveness you do. Yes, people will fly out of town and run to you if you specialize in a niche column of tattooing. Like some artists kill it in black and grey, whereas other artists in simply color or neo-traditional styles. You even have some niche tattoo artists who specialize in prison style with hardcore outlines and more street culture themes. Single needles, homemade tatt guns, and homemade ink without no colors.

This style development is essential and the same signature style celebrity tattoo artist mastered. Whereas they state their own prices hourly, piece-by-piece, or by the inches and sizes of the tattoo. They do this tactic by merely demand once they set it in stone. These celebrity inkmaster get hot afterwards they developed their unique style of specialization. They do not just become tattoo artist and automatically blow up on the tattoo infamous world scene. They get traffic and build traction thru their style development they deploy. A lot of them is perfectionist and do sick tattoos and portraits that look 3-dimensional, with great detail.

Now if your next question is how to develop your signature style? No need to probe and rattle your brain. I'll teach you how to start on developing your style and owning your own tattoo signature. Exercising and focusing on a certain style is good. However, you need a focal point and challenge strategies with doing new things and styles to always be learning. The secret gift is to start off with what you like to do. Your passions and favorite themes you like to do. Your passions and favorite themes you like to tattoo. Don't be afraid to integrate styles and doing different color transitions or concoctions. You cannot just limit yourself to what comes the easiest work to tattoo on your clients. You must look at what style you do your best work on. What pieces look immaculate on your canvas with a helluva mind-blowing result and excited overwhelmed faces with emotional responses. Sustainability is key, too. You need to be able to nail that same piece and style consecutively and perpetually. It must be a consistency style and quality to maintain, if you want to be validated as a stylist inker. You have to master your signature style first before you solidify it. Then once other people recognize it, that will be your stamp of approval that will put you in your only lane.

Remember to keep trying different styles, things, and methods to master your unique craft you wish to develop. Next is vision. You can create a unique incredible vision of style and theme you want to incorporate and articulate, bringing it to life. You can learn and teach yourself any combination of unique collective style accordingly with lots of practice and dedicated time. If you not devoted truly to finessing your craft by means of time and lots of practice development of the art of perfection, then you would fail, or not get the best exclusive results it takes for mastery. They say you are an expert in anything if you put in over 10,000 hours, which is a little shy of 14 months precisely. It takes most artists 24 to 36 months to develop their signature style on average. Therefore it's no rush. However, you must practice to be able to create your vision. Being a creative and a visionary you have to have a process to enable you to implement your plan of actions. Along with your focal points of achievement. It is good to have big visions of creativity and collaborating themes because you can truly be the next new trendy style of tattooing that people prefer and demand in highly popular demographics. Don't listen to the naysayers or the people who think your ideas of new styles or integrating an old traditional style with an urban element is crazy or isn't going to work because it's not possible or normally. So what if it's not the norm or orthodox, you must do what you feel will work best for you and execute. Never mind haters who doubt your craft, bring you down or negative comments. Even if they think your visions of creative styles are too peculiar and bizarre, you need to disregard and ignore them as much as possible. Use their negative feedback as a positive, and fuel to push your creative vision forward and develop your specialized style of tatting. Be relentless.

Next you will want to use a method formula of creating your own community thru that one unique style you desire. Even if others not in your shop or demographics you're tatting like or want it. You build a community around your style. Look for your audience even if it's real niche. Once you make that connection by tapping into that small niche crowd, you will be buzzing and build within that community by demand with exponential growth. This method of formulating is called reverse engineering. By doing things inside out or in reverse by picking apart the metrics, data, or operation of how it works can be a hack of implementation and mechanics 101. Just like that old saying of "if you take the car engine apart and mark all the parts you can easily place it back together then." It's all called reverse engineer or reverse policy. Therefore by sticking to your guns style of tatting that you want to be your developed signature style hands down, you simply cultivate your crowd, then blossom within your demands and network as you lay down amazing work and creative mind-blowing styles. Building a community around your specialization of tatting, you must find the right audience to tap into their market for your style and creative craft exclusively.

You have to have not just passion, you have to have an appetite for development. Yes, you have to be hungry for it. Not just eager. Remember people and ideas will knock you down. However, if you have an artistry appetite, you have to cut all your cords that binds you to failure, fear, fatigue, etc., that stops you from perfecting your craft of development. If anything or anybody stops you from putting in that time and working on your style development you want to formulate, let it go or them go, no doubts. Your dreams, your goals and mission is first and will not nurture themselves or come to fruition.

It's all about how bad you want it regardless your conditions or despite your time. You can reorganize your time and really prioritize what's first and importance of your craft. For example of another specialization, I know a tattoo artist that offers a unique style of service and has his own market and a captivated audience he helped grow. His style is black and grey tatts and mainly portraits. However, his new niche that he specializes in is memorial tattoos of loved ones' portraits that passed away sudden. Now yes, I know you saying you know of a million tattoo artists that offer the same black and grey style with killer portraits that's spot-on the photo verbatim. However, you may not know a tatt artist with this type of added element, though, which is that he incorporates actually loved ones' ashes. He uses the ashes mixed in with the tattoo ink. He does not use the whole ashes of the urn. He only dabs enough to mix into the ink, like a dash of salt or a pinch. Most people feel like their loved one will always be a part of them not from just being inked in blood but with their ashes too. I've seen his audience and his own lane and style he tatts in. I'm pretty sure everyone he told around his shop, workplace, or friends and family laughed, dismissed his idea, telling him forget about it. Or it'll never work because it's too weird, taboo, and would get a single person to sign up to do that with their loved one's ashes and actually pay you for your services. Now he's booked up every moth and have other tatt artist copycats biting off his unique style of incorporation. It's probably 20 artists in every city now that offer this specialized style that they discovered from someone else's development, dedication, and time sought or passion project and special vision. Now I'm not saying you cannot use other tattoo artists' styles, traits, or trademarks. It's just best if you develop your own and keep freestyling ideas and trying different concoction to finesse. Eventually something will stick exclusively for you to own as your own signature style. Then you can brand it and as you being the first one to incorporate and bring to the big board. You rather let someone bite your style than you being known for biting someone else's style. That's why it's essential to develop your own style and best to own your own style of tattoo work.

Energy flows where attention goes. Always remember the solution to your problems are from within your own headspace you create singular. Don't let people make it plurally. Now the example I just mentioned about this unique artist that developed his black and grey style with ashes of deceased loved ones was an eye-opener meant for inspiration to you. You can learn thru this lesson that you can not just only develop your own style with hard work and dedication, that you can also use different and added elements like he did. It's no limitations set in stone on tattoos or certain rules of engagement. Remember it's all a creative art form and practice. Don't be afraid to add different elements, bring different elements to the table, mix and create them. Don't give up on development and finding your own style, the beginning is always hard. Stop, give it a rest, then get back at it and formulating your skillset, sparking creativity of style and elements.

Next after you finally found a style that fit you and you mastered thru intense development, you need to name it. That's correct. Pick out a name to fit and stick especially 20 years from now. It must go good with your actual style and corroborate with it. Even your theme or element to your style should coincide with the name. The name of your style can be extreme or not match at all if you so like. However, if it match or rhythm, it will ring. If it's more catchy it will hook someone and be easier to remember. Remember once you name it, you own it and have to abide by it the duration.

- Chapter 4 -

"Your Portfolio"

Your portfolio should be your profession and prestige. All tattoo artist beginners to veterans should have an active portfolio. A proper portfolio should provide exhibits and canvas you tatted. Preferably your portfolio should have mainly photos of your fresh tattoos after you finished and cleaned from your clients. This is a way to display some of your best work and sick pieces that display and perpetuate your style further. With a portfolio you use it as a reference of your work, skillset, and style. Most of all experience and trust from a client or new potential clients.

First allow me to educate you on what a portfolio is and why it's helluva necessary. It's just like your work résumé prior. By definition a portfolio is a portable case for papers or drawings. Most tattoo artists use photo albums to showcase their talent and best prior projects. Or you can look up tattoo portfolio albums/ cases online of all sizes if you would like. Another defined meaning of portfolio is the securities held by an investor, like people on Wall Street, like stock markets and brokers. They always advise people to have a diverse portfolio. You may have heard this term used exactly before. This is why I do agree with diversity and diversifying your portfolio.

By diverse portfolio you have different and more content which more is better. More to display and gaining more potential clients, fans, and tapping into a new different community of tatts. More demographics means more customers across the board, which all tattoo artists need to stay working, active, and paid. You don't want your tattoo hand to go cold like some feet. You want your tattoo hand to be hot and go strong! If you go from a full-time tattoo artist to a side job tattoo gig artist, you are going backwards and need to switch up your content with more diversity. People do not want the same boring tatts or the tattoos similar to everyone else. A tattoo artist should go from starting off with being a side job tattoo gig to full-fledged tatt artist full-time and booked up.

Now the next question is how do you diversify your portfolio correctly? First you need to organize and sequence it with your content. You need to convey your styles of tattoos like neo-tradition, wild, color, animate, or black and grey. Then incorporate your specialization styles and niche work. Again, you must be able to display your best work which you have to be consistently staying in pattern, all lines spot-on, and color and shading transitions on point, too. People are judging your portfolio the minute they open it up to browse thru it.

How to align your portfolio is putting your best work in its class or style of tattoos in sections. Maybe 3 to 5 pages of finished pieces to display at a time. Then you sync the next style and follow this same pattern throughout your portfolio. An example is you'd put your tattoo style and subjects all in one section. Next you follow it up with a different tattoo style and subjects. Like doing all your black and grey portraits and pieces, then displaying all your color, traditional, or animate cartoon styles and subjects until your portfolio is aligned and complete. You can use this concept for multiple portfolios. You also can use one photo album per each style and subject for your portfolio. Let's say you want to display 5 to 6 styles in your portfolio and have a lot of great content, then you would want to use 5 to 6 different albums for your portfolio. However, just let your guests and potential clients know that each photo album only displays a particular tattoo style and subject, and that you have 5 or however many more that consist of your portfolio.

Your portfolio is what connects your customers to your artwork. It's the factor that gives your artwork and tatt skills power and validation. The patterns can all change and all the trendy tattoo subjects. However, your tattoo skills will showcase without diminished value. You can even evolve it with more added value to your portfolio.

Next is not to confuse your tattoo pattern books or folders for your clients to look at and brose thru for an actual portfolio. Those tattoo books you see when you go into an actual tattoo shop is specific for your selection. To pick out a tattoo pattern you want to get tatted on you. Or it's to give you an idea and feedback of what combos you can mix up to tattoo on you. This is not your portfolio, though. You can get all these common styles of tattoo patterns and subjects for your shop or booklets to fill online or at local tattoo supplies outlets. However, make sure you clear and direct with signs or labels to your selection patterns book versus portfolios with finished best work displayed.

To index your portfolio you can snap pics from your phone and save them, then pick out later from your best or favorite ones. You can use different printing apps and options like the Walgreens app or Kinko's. They give you the options of print and pick-up. With your mobile device you can even use the filters, special features, and captions to display your tattoo finish results style and work. Hashtags or using the style of tatting name to identify to your audience and potential clients. Also if you have a printer at the shop or home work space, you can print out right there on the spot and add to your portfolio folder or album to display.

Another prime way to showcase your portfolio and artwork is post on all social platforms like Facebook, Instagram, Twitter, and Snapchat. Posting is a great marketing ploy and you can connect with or reach millions, which we will get into further in chapters to come. Displaying online is a great tool to use for portfolio. At your shop it's limited to how many people per day see your portfolio. Whereas, online people can review your portfolio at a higher rate per day, equivalent to 3 to 4 weeks at your studio. Therefore, it's very beneficial and expandable. It gives you more exponential growth with fans, clientele, and other artists. Your structure of your portfolio shouldn't be messy or careless and effortless. Trust me, presentation is everything and nobody wants to surf thru a tacky portfolio. A mental note, make sure your portfolio is sharp and what you yourself would like to browse thru intact.

Note that these are all ways to help you diversify your portfolio, similar to how stock investors do. Another element you can use to diversify your tattoo portfolio is to display a section of your best cover-up tatt work.

In displaying a cover-up section in your portfolio is totally optional and up to you as an artist, especially if you are not good at doing cover-ups as an artist. Most artists will not dare touch another prior artist's work. Or they simply will not attempt to do a cover-up. They do not like challenges or accept the challenge because the fear of the cover-up looking worse, or not being able to deliver the task with promising results for the client's satisfaction. If a client comes in for a cover-up and cannot get it covered up properly and it still shows a little, they will be upset because now they have to come off more cash to get it covered up once again. It's a tricky and sticky situation for some artists. I'll show you how to do proper cover-ups in the next chapter effectively.

To do this cover-up section in your portfolio, you can add the before and after photos if you like. Preferably side-by-side pics looks better than pics displayed from top to bottom. The visual effect helps and looks way better for your portfolio fit and imagery like magic. Or you can just display your best cover-ups without the before photos. You can simply label them and their sections of your portfolio, or enclosed photos using your filters or captions from your mobile devices. Another tip and piece of advice, if organizing your portfolio is too complex to get it just right, you can have a woman do it. Females are the organizers and decoratives to frame it with a collage and beautiful sequence. Not saying guys cannot do the same or incapable. You should consider hiring a female or reach out to one with great taste. If you can't afford to pay her, ask for her opinion or consultant. You will go further using this practice as well. Your portfolio and its design is whatever you make it. If you're a woman tattoo artist or an inspiring tatt artist and having trouble executing your portfolio properly, you, too, can go to a girlfriend for advice and overview, or you can hire another woman to consult and help you formulate your portfolio for the best eye-catching imagery.

If your portfolio is not getting the turnover results you need to sustain you as an active tattoo artist, you may need to be open-minded and open for suggestion on your content and consistency. You will not be able to build a community or vast clientele. Also you can get typecasted as a tattoo artist within one lane. That lane can be glued to some of your crappy or beginner stages of work. You cannot pick or choose what tattoos you are most known for. However, you can set up your plate correct from the jumpstart so you do not have to offer bad content that you have hiccups on or inconsistency on your line work and small details. Therefore, you have the right opportunity to put forth your best work. If you are closed-minded you will be blinded at the perception of what you see versus what others see. Then you cannot rearrange your portfolio because you can't blow up and become a renowned tatt artist off of what only you like and think the people would like. You have to display in your portfolio what people like, demanding, or buzzing about. For instance if you like tatting suns, spaceships, and butterflies, then display in each tattoo style throughout your portfolio from color to black and grey. Versus if you tap in online and pay attention to all the feedback and people's demands, comments, and trends on your pages or social media platforms.

Your portfolio should be pleasant to look at, enjoyable and inspiring. You want people to be moved and inspired to get that similar tatt done. By being singular and not plural tattoos, you run the risk of being boring, bland, or too simplistic. Again, please model your portfolio in the best of best from subject, style, colors, niche, or cover-ups. They all need to be crispy and clean finish pieces.

The last suggestion in your portfolio is the option of showing whole persons smiling with their new tattoo. Or just close-up canvas pieces. Maybe you can do a concoction of full-body pieces and close-up canvas pieces both. The full-body image and display of an actual person versus a piece on a part of a person can help convince people that it will look great on them, too. Influencing them to want that tattoo or that right spot to tatt. It also displays placements, too.

- Chapter 5 -

"Building Clientele"

Now that you have full understanding of what a portfolio is, how to lay yours out precisely, and the importance of it, the next step in this chapter is the key to building clientele. Building clients is significant in a pillar of being a tattoo artist. All of these chapters in *How to Tattoo* is not only just showing you how to tattoo and textbook education, it's also one big cipher. It all coincides.

The word "client" means a person who engages the professional services of another or patron, customer, dependent. Clientele is a body of clients and especially customers. To build your clientele is to increase, enhance, or enlarge. The aim is to have a focus goal on building clients and optimizing within that fashion. It's no cheat sheet in building or growing clientele and your tattoo business. It is a process and method. I'll give you a guideline to set your building clientele foundation and then how to perpetuate that method and continue to scale.

Building your audience and your tattoo brand is different from building customers. You do not just want brand awareness, you want the clientele to actually get your tattoo service and pay for your services. You want to get sales and close on your clients. Having a high close rate or turnover rate is how you scale. We will get into tattoo brand building in the chapters to come also. However, you need to know there is a distinct difference and not to mix the two up. Building an audience can help you get potential clients thru awareness and branding or following. However, building clientele is people that want tattoos, that is looking for better tatt artists, and always working on more parts of their body to tatt. These people are the ones you want to focus on. They are your targeted clientele that you know is looking to pay you for your services, and to help fill in different parts of their canvas. Men and women of all ages above 18 years old all want ink done. You are focusing on building and connecting with people who have that tattoo bug, tattoo fever, or that simply love ink and got to always have more and looking for that next piece. Tattoos are highly addicting for people and if they get one, their second one is soon to follow. However, not everyone that gets a tattoo will like it and get another one. Especially, people that do not like the sting and pain duration. You want to have a high conversion and comeback rate. You want to build repeated and frequent clientele that knows you on a first name or tattoo artist name basis, including frequent your shop or shops on a basis, too.

By building you want to create gradually by optimizing your clientele with doing great work and customer service skills. Be friendly and having a nice and clean safe environment. Your customer experience with you and at the shop should be great and always one to remember. It's important that the artist create the environment to provide an ultimate tattoo experience. Especially if it's a first-timer at your shop, tattoo, or you being the artist to tatt on them, too. To provide a comfort experience and for them to feel welcome and want to come back again for your services. You want them to show off your tattoo work and shop work so they can brag and tell a friend or two. These are ways how you build clientele through referrals, which people will come in, including first-timers and state that Suzy sent them and they seen the coral fish you did colorful on her and they really liked it, and so on. Building on quality and trust is another key element to keeping clientele coming and growth time and time again. All while spreading telling a friend and sharing their tattoo amazing experience.

It is the similar experience at a barber shop or a hair & nail salon. You build a connection and relationship with your clients. Trust, quality service creates lifetime customer bonds, which is the aim. Therefore, you don't just let anyone cut your hair or do your hairstyle and nails. You got with that same barber and stylist you know trust and formed that service client and professional bond with. You have to use this same concept and do some reverse engineering, put yourself in your client's shoes. Then think what will your customer want, appreciate, and value that will give an ultimate experience for them to come back again or to engagement for a lifetime customer versus lifestyle customer.

Do simple steps to make your customers happy and comfortable with a great tattoo trusting experience. Regardless of challenges may come. You have to have passion and energy into building clientele consistently. You must have confidence at an all-time high with a friendly welcoming smile on your face to be able to execute day in and day out with generating clients and keeping them coming back.

Building a devoted client is he or she coming back for you to sleeve them down or tatt them from head-to-toe. You do get clients that specific only want one tattoo artist exclusively to do all their pieces. You don't want to cross your fingers to get lucky for one of these type clients to fall in your lap. No, instead you want to develop the building process with every potential client to be a one exclusive artist for their whole entire canvas. You can do this by laying your best hand forward, creating all-around customer service and experience. It's not just your tatting skillset because it's tattoo shops and flyers everywhere you tun. You need to have customer service skills, customer acquisition and social skills. If you are not a people person, you are in the wrong skill of trade. It doesn't matter if you're an introvert or not. You simply must obtain people skills and maintain your tactics you put in place. You always keep them customer service skills in play. Clients is first before anything, without them there is no tattoo artist, shop, or cash flow.

You can create your own list of customer skills, service, and mannerisms that you use and implement daily from open to close.

Reputation equals implementation methods and practices. Make sure you do your checklist every day until that becomes routine and norm habit of people skills and quality customer service with building clientele tactics. Market yourself and tatt experience for your clients to be encaptured to your shop and services rendered with customer engagement.

Engagement building wins time and time again. You build fans, too. Then they will definitely got to share their experience with a friend. Plus the great quality of your clean tattoo work and safe clean practice. It's important to note that fans help build clientele and vast your audience thru boasting likes and stoked obsession. Especially thru word of the mouth. That's just like them telling their friends online to check out this new or shocking video which all the clicks boost the status and algorithm to be a viral sensation. This is essentially called shock value. Building clientele unexpected thru someone else. Then with forward clientele coming, you build a community and listen to them. Especially all the feedback, because that is a key to growth client building and longevity. Most of all to evolve your customer building and client relationships. Remember to pay attention to any demands. Customer demands in person or on social media. This is how you get better and achieve exponential growth. It's also how you expand your mind and method.

A building clientele skill I use and showcase it a common friendly greeting to everyone that enters the shop. A simple salutation like "hello" or saying "Welcome to the Tattoo Shop" greeting with a pleasant smile planted brightly on my face along with the rest of the shop artists that are not currently busy working on a tattoo. Someone feels more comfortable and welcome into a place or new environment when they are greeted correctly with a cheerful smile from the whole place. It's a warm smile and contagious, makes all potential clients light up inside.

Next I approach them with a handshake and ask what are they looking for today, a tattoo or piercing. Then I offer them an option between if they want to look at our portfolios or booklets of tattoo patterns. My third option is to ask them if they would like our free offer of consultant without no commitments.

Part of scaling clientele is helping them and structuring them without no money down or getting paid. By you merely advising is part of the job. You can't expect to get paid for that. You not coaching, you are advisory only. In this line of business you will find from experience there are a lot of indecisive people coming into your shop left and right, switching ideas or changing their mind. You'll definitely need patience, a crucial element in dealing with building clientele. You may get a new client that picks out a tattoo pattern and changes it at the last minute. Or switches after you placed the stencil on and machine set ready to go. They simply change their minds and pull out or back out of the deal. Fear of getting a tattoo or coming in buzzed and drunk all play factors when client building and development process with patience. You have to be patient with them all because you never know which one will come back to your shop being a repeat customer or potentially a lifetime customer. Therefore, patience is definitely a virtual and a given plus in the art form of tatting.

Another way artists build clientele is they offer special services or do harder tasks that other artists refuse. Especially cover-ups. It's challenging, however, how to properly cover up tatts. You must first pick the best pieces that will fill the canvas more bigger to fit. You need to keep trying the stencils with different options for your clients to choose from. Most clients say they don't care what you cover it up with, just long as it's covered up completely. People can simply get the tattoo removed, but it's more sitting sessions than a cover-up. Next you want to be able to collage the cover-up into the new tattoo without being too dark. Also no transparency. Avoid all heavy blur dark spots or patches. You do not want to have an all-black solid shade block Band-Aid over as a cover-up either. You may get away with a few lines of a cover-up showing when blending it with the new lines. However, a cover-up shouldn't be noticeable. If you can see it, then you didn't achieve customer satisfaction or get the job done correct and will lose a comeback customer.

Therefore, don't be rushing or doing quick effortless jobs. No one-night stands, marry your customers, and create lifetime value. Have your social media presence, too, to add value by showing your customer service experience for potential clientele. Optimism wins wars and beats all. That concludes this chapter. Now the framework and formulation building is ready.

- Chapter 6 -

"Mobile Tatting"

Now that you have learnt the basics of tatting 101 and developed your style and formulated your portfolio attractively, it's time to take your craft on the go and expand your reach. Most people starting out as tattoo artists cannot get directly hired at a shop or get work because they don't have years of experience. You will be denied due to lack of experience, practice, and being a household name. Especially if you never worked at other shops on your tattoo résumé. You maybe cannot get that reference or referral you need to get into a shop for work and permanent residency. Especially for hire and trust.

Therefore, you may not have that opportunity to get a best start into a shop. However, that does not mean you have to sit around lying dormant until the phone rings after a shop artist quits. You can keep your tatt hand hot by going out there mobile looking for work. Doing house calls, pulling up to people's homes. Go to tattoo expos and set up your booth or workstation and equipment. Also go on call work for shops when people don't show, or they get too busy and flooded with clients. You can go on tattoo party buses or home tattoo parties. I have even pulled up to tattoo hotel parties, too, using these mobilizing tactics. Extras and being hired for extra help is part of being mobile and staying relevant in your tattoo local community. You have to be willing to tatt on the road.

To be transparent mobile tatting is not a mobile tattoo app or virtual tatting. Mobil tattoo is being able to travel to clients, events, or places and shops. This is essential to be mobile and enable your services. You can even expand your network traveling out of state or flying overseas, too. You can have your own mobile trailer that you use as your tattoo station. You can find mobile trailers custom for mobile tatt stations that can hold all your equipment, tatt chair with a sink and generator in it all online. If you do choose to buy a mobile tattoo trailer, make sure your ROI (return on investment) outweighs the cost and will pay off. For example, if you don't have enough clientele or a place to go to set up shop and park your mobile trailer at. Again, this is a mobile tattoo trailer that you can tatt clients inside of. It's not an actual mobile trailer home. These tattoo mobile trailers you can attach to the back of your truck or car to haul it around from location to location. Some of these mobile tattoo trailers brand new can be very expensive. Especially for starters with barely enough cash flow. I would suggest looking into a used pre-owned mobile tattoo trailer. Get it financed or workout a deal to make payments thru a contract. Still if you cannot afford to do this or have no direct means, you can scratch the mobile trailer idea and take an Uber or bike to do house calls with all your supplies, sanitation, and machine. You do not have to have extravagant means to do mobile tatting. Simply use the resource you have within or only outsource of what you can afford.

If you choose to carry around your tattoo equipment in a box or backpack, be careful with theft prevention and safety sanitation practices. You want to make sure you have enough wipes, cleaning supplies, needles along with everything you need and would normally have tatting at home. Make sure the space you tatting at is clean with airflow. The environment you enter or go to has to be sanitary and safe, including the sterilization of everything in that space, chair, or area you tatting in. Remember, being in a foreign environment or someone else's space you still risk infections or bloodborne pathogens spreading. Therefore, you still need to take all the necessary proper precautions on the road as you would at your normal place of tatting or workstation.

Even if you are currently employed at the shop or running your own tattoo practice doesn't mean you cannot have a side hustle with mobile tatting. You can expand and extend your services, too. There is no rule that says you cannot do both. Long as you have the time and energy after your daytime tattoo job, you can definitely achieve mobile tatting after hours, or on the weekends. In the tattoo business anything is possible to implement if you dedicate the time and resources into it.

To enable yourself to do mobile tatting and extra odd jobs, you need to have your transportation down pat. Transportation is the number-one priority to figure out a constant source and means of transportation. Ask yourself how are you going to get to a potential client or spot event to tattoo and back to your destination. Transportation if you do not have a vehicle. You need to make sure you have all your core bases covered first with transportation to be mobile before you offer your services, make arrangements, and commit to mobile jobs, or promoting yourself. Again, you can use all your local transportation methods around you from bus, light rail, subway, train, or rideshares. You can even have friends and family chauffeur you around, too. Just make sure you have pre-agreements and they have a heads-up notification prior to the time you need that ride to your tattoo locations. Make sure they have a clear schedule and time free to transport you accordingly. You can tip friends and family for their transport services. Maybe even offer them gas money if they don't have an e-car. Most friends and family help you out the kindness of their hearts and don't want your money. However, it's still a great practice to tip them still anyway. It's good measure. Especially if you use them regularly or need them again. The only time it's not suitable to tip any of your drivers is if you are tatting for free or at a charity event.

Next we will shift into promo. Promoting your mobile tattoo services. The first step is to make your services known and reachable to all. How you do this is starting off with promoting yourself with flyers and business cards. You can go online to VistaPrint to get a great deal on business cards. You also can make your flyers online, too.

I personally would go to Kinko's to design and print my flyers, make them all colors and appealing. Also I'd do my tattoo card designs, too. When doing your mobile tattoo service flyers or business cards, you can keep it simple and basic designs. You don't need to make it complex and too time-consuming. It does not have to look effortless either.

The main things you need on a business card and flyer to promote your mobile tattoo service is your name, brand, contact info like a mobile number, email. You can also put your social media handles for contact or simply to see your work, like your Snapchat and TikTok handles to see your current tattoo videos and pics. Your Instagram and Facebook if you have them, too. Remember everything is one big circle of promo and branding that ciphers perpetually.

You can even include your tattoo logo or signature trademark. This is if you have one designed. Like if you have a sword and a skull for your brand logo of sword and bones, you would find a place on the flyer or card. The logo or your design placement do not have to be centered or in a specific spot. It is totally up to you. It's your card, flyer, and mobile services. Design how you please or see fit. Just remember, don't place your flyers or hand out your business cards outside your transportation limits. You cannot go outside your reach or transport means. You will run the risk of people leaving you with bad reviews or a bad business name while you attempting to build clients and start up your mobile services to your community. You must not take on jobs that you cannot fulfill.

You can go to shopping malls or plazas parking lots to pass out flyers or put into car windshields where it's permitted. If your city, state, or that shopping center don't allow loitering or soliciting customers, you should be good. You still would want to check your local laws and get permission by asking those establishments first before you go passing flyers from car to car.

Be creative when passing out flyers or business cards. Look for new or alternative methods around your area and expand your mind by innovating more. Make it interesting, have some fun with it.

I would go outside of bards, bowling alleys, and barbershops to pass out flyers. I would go to fast food joints handing out my tattoo mobile card. Some establishments even to their employee on the clock. I'd always smile and shake their hands after I hand them a business card with my credentials and tell them if they don't use it, tell a friend or give it to a friend looking for some new tatt work. Therefore, always work your magic and charm to make a helluva first impression. It's all about leaving a mark and your grind. Passion, drive, education, and the power of positive energy will take you a long way in any quest or profession you seek.

Lastly, in this mobile tatting chapter, I would like to leave you with another additional option or bonus tool you can use to spread your mobile tatting hustle or grindwork. This is doing a party bus rental. A rental is also a great option of any transportational means or car you seeking. Especially if you have a theme to cause to follow.

It can be a bachelor tattoo party, a birthday tattoo party, or even a pool tattoo party. These are all themes or causes that you use as an underlying factor and premise for your event planning and promo behind, which you can pull up to any of these options you organize and drive traffic to mobile.

This is how I did my party bus rentals. I first Google local exotic party buses. Once I found one I liked and compared rates, I went to meet the owner, secured a deposit down for the rental. Then I established a relationship with the owner, which help me get a better and lower rate for future rentals. Then I would make Facebook and Instagram flyers about a Super Bowl Tattoo Party bus Friday thru Sunday and listed all locations and park times. After 3 hours in one place and doing a few mediocre tattoos not too complex, we would drive the party bus, celebrate and blast music. It was a success, of course, and work. Next I did Spring Break Tattoo Party bus theme. Another success, plus I had made my own tattoo party bus merch like T-shirts and hats. You can do all of this to be creative and inspired.

- Chapter 7 -

"Start-Up & Branding"

This is the fun part of the book because you can be crafty and use your creative power in the process of innovation and business. This chapter we will show you how to start up your own tattoo business from A-to-Z to open up your own shop one day. Also enable you to hire or fire your own employee artist. Then we will go over branding and how to market yourself all in one.

The first initial step is to pick out a name and a logo. Logos are optional. However, make sure your tattoo shop name fits your brand and theme if you have one, too. Your brand name and tattoo shop trade name should be the same or co-exist and integrate.

Once you pick out the name you wish to call your shop and tattoo brand, you go downtown to register it. Every state and county is different with different guidelines or stipulations. Therefore, you need to go online, check your local listing. Typically you go to a government building like the Secretary of State, Chamber of Commerce, Department of Revenue, or business registry state buildings. You would fill out an application for a trade name or fictitious business name, then pay the registration fee. Each county and state registration trade name fee is different. Especially if you do this at USPTO (United States Patent & Trademark Office) for your logo fees. If you want to register your tattoo brand logo, you would file a local trademark form of the design logo or the logo name. For instance, let's use Nike as an example. They have the written word Nike logo or the check mark sign logo or they use them both together one on top of each other.

When registering your trademark logo, you usually need to provide 3 copies of how your logos are used, like a business card, or on a flyer, they need for their hard copy files. However, it has to be digitally formatted. No handwritten logos in pens, pencils, or color pencils and crayons. If it is in handwritten or drafted text, it will be rejected and they will not accept your trademark form or filing fees.

The next step is to get your business license to sell merchandise and tattoo out of your shop doing cash transactions. Again, some states and counties do not need or require a tattoo license. Whereas, other states and counties only require a tattoo work permit. Some states allow you to just register your tattoo shop and pay for your tax privilege license.

You need to do your local searches again to find out where you go to register your business license. Like the Department of Revenue Business and Services section. Request their TPIN (tax privilege identification number) to sell merchandise and do business out of your shop. You pay the filing fee with the business license application. If you have to register your tattoo permit or license, too, do them both at the same time. You can search for all your state and county prerequisites for your tattoo license. You may even need a certain amount of work hours and a safety and sanitation course beforehand, too.

The next step is to go to the IRS.gov website and file for an EIN (employer identification number), this is for federal taxes and to be able to pay your employees, and do payroll and taxes. Once you get your EIN after filling out the paperwork, it's usually free to file. This is the company social security number basically. This enables and supports your workforce and establishment.

Some states and counties make you place a classified ad in the paper or online for 60 to 90 days before issuing a trade name certificate. You're required to put people on notice after you paid your filing fees. If your state don't require all this, then you are free to take your trade name certificate to a bank or a credit union to set up a business account for your tattoo shop. Also, take your EIN and TPIN if they request both and your driver's license or ID card.

Most business accounts you can apply online and they would want you to email all those documents and proof. All starter business accounts usually have a $200 to $500 deposit or stipulations that you must keep a bare minimum of $200 to $500 in that account at all times. However, if you do your research, some are less deposits or free. Especially if you already have a regular checking or savings with that bank or credit union because you have bank history and trust. This is also the same method you get business or bank loans thru that same history, trust, and credit building.

This next step is very important to put your thought, research, and best decision in. It is getting your tattoo LLC (limited liability company) behind your company and brand. I would highly recommend this LLC practice thru experience. It is totally up to you. First, I'll explain to you the difference between obtaining an LLC, S-Corp., Inc., or operating as a sole proprietorship.

A sole proprietorship is you running your business as a sole owner exclusively. With a sole proprietorship, you are not protected from risk management, liability, and civil or class action suits, which these lawsuits someone or groups of people at your establishment can sue you as an individual and as an entity. Therefore, the judge can tap into your business account, personal account, and relinquish funds. Or you can be sued and lose your house or car, too. You are not protected. Versus an LLC which protects you as an entity where you cannot be sued for personal assets. An LLC is risk management on the other hand, but not required. It fits a lot of microbusinesses and starters.

An S-Corp. is a small corporation. Some people get their LLC and run it as an actual S-Corp. Or the last option is to get your Inc., which is an incorporation. Incs are usually for big companies with lots of employees or for organizations. Typically you wouldn't do a tattoo Inc. However, you can do any of these options you choose. I am not a lawyer. You should see legal consultant.

To register your LLC, S-Corp, or Inc., you can go online to LegalZoom. It will have a list of options, fees, and instructions. Some sites have free consultations via Skype or telephonic. Fees range from $99 to $500-plus, depends what direction and package you choose for your business. You can also check your local listing corporation commission or corporation registry building in your state and file the apps. On LegalZoom it's easier and convenient. You have a lawyer that reps you and files the paperwork and lets you know when the process is over. The process usually takes 90 days after the lawyer files a classified ad in the paper publicly. Then after every year, you have to pay usually a renewal fee from $100 to $300. If you miss your renewal fee, you will have to refile and pay them $400 for a late file fee typically. Therefore, it's essential to do your homework and research. Feel free to shop around online. Get different consultants and rates, then you decide the betterment.

Now that you are all registered and ready to open up shop legit, you search for your first building. You have two options: Leasing a building for rent space monthly, or second choice, to buy a building flat out. To finance a building new or old, you need to have great credit and a huge down payment, or have the capital thru other sources like family and friends, settlements, or huge savings. You may can only afford a small hole in the wall at first, but it's still yours and a start.

Having your own shop is an opportunity and how you handle it by running a successful practice with great marketing. Or a bad practice and a flop, causing you to shut down shop for good before you can excel. You should lease a building to test out if you have what it takes to run and maintain a tattoo shop successfully, including thru a few stress tests of full capacity.

Search online for buildings or space for lease according to your monthly budget without stretching it. Then make sure your location is everything and not compromised from the jump. Like you don't want to lease a space next to a pig processing plant and your clients smell poop and stink at your shop. You want to find spots where a lot of people frequent and interact. Like in shopping plazas, by pool halls, bowling alleys, bars, even next to food joints, too. Be very smart about selection of area and choice of your surroundings.

Once you find the exact building, meet with the owner and do a walkthrough and have an inspection before you put down the deposit or sign the lease agreement. Usually the lease agreements can be from month-to-month, 6 months, or a year lease contract.

Next, it is time to deck your first shop out and buy shop equipment, supplies, chairs, booths, and mirrors. This is the fun part to search and have your friends and family help you decorate accordingly to your brand and theme. With this you can buy new or used stuff. I go on Facebook Marketplace or eBay for better tattoo chairs, tables, and full wall mirrors. I go to Sam's

Club to buy shop cleaning and sanitation supplies by bulk and wholesale deals.

You can go into other shops and use their same model layout of operation. Implementation model after other experts to complete your initial layout with your own styles and twist.

Now let's get into a business plan. You do not have to have one to start up and register your tattoo business. However, a business plan is a great practice and acts as your business road map and operations plan. It's nothing like hands-on experience thru trial and errors. The plus is a business plan can enable you to get a tattoo business loan because most loans require a business plan. They want to know what, when, and how are you going to pay them back. You can Google business plan templates or workshops to walk you through the business plan so you can fill in the blanks and create your own. Always make sure you leave an extra 15 percent revenue for overhead. That's for all the unexpected things that pop up at the shop that needs fixing or emergencies you did not plan for or include into your business plan because you couldn't foresee extra expense. Trust me as an expert from experience and take that tip as a jewel.

Set up your cash register and get a Square to swipe cards for payments. Then get you bookkeepers like QuickBooks to organize your payment structure and help you document all your sales and transactions. Once you get your business sale license, you will have to document all your monthly and quarterly earnings to turn in for taxes at the end of year and file, too. Therefore, your day-to-day transactions need to be accounted for. Merch and services.

Finally, place some ads for employees or find artists online that's dope and call them in for interviews. See all their work referrals and look thru their portfolio thoroughly. Then lay out all your rules, regulations, and expectations. Be clear about if they didn't perform they will be fired from failure to meet your shop demands.

How you set up rent from your employees is renting them out a workstation, booth, or chair weekly after you hire them. You divide a ratio of your lease of the building, then set a price off that. If you have four chairs or workstations, that's four employees that can rent them out from you and occupy them to the fullest possibility. Then you tell all four of your tatt artists $400 per week. Next you multiply $400 x 4, which is $1,600 per week from all four artists. Now you multiply $1,600 x 4, which equals $6,400 per month of employee revenue. Then you subtract your actual shop's rent. If your monthly lease agreement is $2,500, you subtract $6,400, which is $3,900 in the green, not including your personal cash flow from tatting your clients, too, or the revenue from a shop body piercer as a feature. You can write a spreadsheet and formulate your own structure. It's endless possibilities. Take a money management course and get shop insurance.

Now that you have that start-up structure and how-to framework step-by-step, we will get into branding. Branding is just like the previous discussion on developing your style and creativity. Well, with branding, you want to use that same touch of inspiration and creativity to build your brand and branding as your marketing. You start off with your mission statement. What is your brand? Then why? What is so different from your brand than the next tattoo shop brand down the street? These are the questions you ask yourself and brainstorm filling in the blank until something fits and matches your theme, background, style, or slogans.

Focus on what you want to be in branding and deliver that time and time again without straying from your message or theme. One mission and branding message. Watching and learning from people's feedback. Create a focus person or shop brand. What do you want to be known for? What do you stand out for more than other brands in the tattoo space? Can you create a new brand in a crowded space, especially with all the renowned brands?

To help you formulate, let's say you came up with 2 written-down concepts and torn between 2 different brand names. Once you named Inks R Us and the other you named Inky. I would go with the shorter one or the catchy name. Anyone that's more impressionable and stands out. If it has more of a ring, it's easier to remember and look up online, which also markets itself. Organic traffic and marketing is the best because you do not have to pay the play for results and potential clients.

Let's say you choose Inky, then your branding message will be "Inky—We ink you from head to toe." This can be your slogan, too.

Then your tattoo brand logo can be a Bic ink pen with a tattoo gun and motor look to it designed like a homemade or jailhouse style single needle tattoo gun. You can swag your logo out and put a grin on the gun and design if you want to. Next you use this as your premise and base of your whole entire tattoo shop brand and banner. Create a buzz and build all your messaging around it. All your branding should lead back to "We ink you from head to toe." Like got ink? Well, you not Inky yet? Come to visit us at our Inky location in person or @Inky.com for your virtual Inky tattoo shop tour. Offer to view all your portfolio and rates. Have an email list and a sign-up sheet. When setting your rates, you can do by the tattoo size or inches. Big time-consuming pieces you can charge per hour or check what other fellow shops charging and choose to give a flat rate, discount, or higher rate. It's all up to you how you market rates with your branding.

Next is brand awareness. How do you let people know about you, your shop brand, and services? First, you need to know who your targeted audience market is. Find your tattoo space and fans or potential clients and tap into them. Social media awareness and presence is mandatory in building a brand.

Grow your brand as a shop and an artist. Having your breakthrough. Use your outlet of what you have to get people to recognize you. Drive forward your vision and brand messaging and believe in yourself and brand. Go viral, live, attack those digital platforms, find more ways to showcase your talent. Again, it's a crowded marketing space, but talent shines through.

Make personal connections. Everybody is your marketer and if they need your tattoo service, they choose you. Make people know you and your brand and get familiar. Awareness is the best marketing tool. Connect with people and they will refer people back to you. If you already got the audience, it's easier to market. Figure out how you can promote to variety and vast people.

However, you need to engage in your marketplace and spread awesomeness. You can pay Facebook or Google Ads, but automation does not work like actualization of engagement and realization. Get clear on what you want, be very detailed, and figure out how to give value to people. Your shop needs customer service and caring about your customer. Online marketing by engaging and add value. Talk to people, comment, and engage online with a simple Hello. Twitter, you can start talking to them first and get to know them virtual first before they come into your shop, mobile services, or events.

Do all social media platforms for your brand awareness. Create all accounts, a Facebook business page promo. Linkedin, Pintrest, Snapchat. Even TikTok to shoot videos, lessons, words and tips, or sessions of your best challenging work.

Even though people cannot be there to engage or gain that tattoo experience, they can still watch you live or your videos. They can comment, like, share, or retweet. The point is you get engagement and feedback to see your pain or PowerPoints to innovate and push a totally different way. That's ROI on social media. Just like sweat equity. It's all you making an investment and building that momentum. Being stern with brand consistency.

Instagram helps with brand awareness to post pics of your tattoo work and shop environment. Twitter you can brand by tweeting all of your locations, news, and specials.

Brand equity and crossbranding is integrating other brands that add value to your brand thru promo or special features, shoutouts or events. Like KFC with Coke crossbranding moves by integrating both their audience in that same food space. Make sure it fits your brand before you integrate other brands with yours and converge followers tapping into others' audience. Check their history online and offline in their community. Take some time with this, don't be so quick to jump in and say Yes! It's okay to say No, because you may be hurting your brand, branding, or brand messaging. Even if people offer to pay you to advertise their tattoo brand, or promo and features, you got to do your homework because it may not work and can push your marketers away and lose more money than you made off of crossbranding.

Lastly, you can do something different and try different marketing ploys or new strategies to make your brand impact. You have to have an open mind within reality and reason. Grow your tattoo business and brand daily. You cannot stop where you are. You must set goals and keep on evolving your brand consistently.

An example is creating a new brand marketing space by starting a new tattoo podcast with your brand. Then you can create the greatest tattoo convo experience where you give up how-tos, tips, bonuses, and feature artists up and coming or renowned artists. You can even add another tattoo artist guest host the tattoo podcast with. This is great marketing and branding because it's tattoo social life that's rich and vivid, people can see their favorite tatt artist. You can become a tattoo personality online and the face of your brand and the marketplace. You can have all your tattoo brand merch in the background, like cups, posters, shirts, joggers, etc. Plus you can wear your own hoodies, hats, or even masks of your brand for promo while viewers watch you on your podcast. You build a following by doing weekly podcasts. Create amazing content. Spread enlightenment, passion, and artist dialogue. You will build your engagement and email list for feedback, acknowledgements and new podcast show ideas to go off of and formulate. Make a vision board.

Lastly, in branding you must show appreciation and gratitude. Show your customers and virtual audience in your market space great appreciation because it goes a long way and has the ability to last longer and have a lasting impact or impression. Finally, with branding it's not just using your head, awareness, and engagement to grow. It's hard work and execution!

- Chapter 8 -

"Customization & Special Features"

Customization is one of the best added elements along with special features for your shop, brand, and style to stay ahead of that curve of regularity. Customize is to build, fit, or alter accordingly to individual specifications. Therefore, all clients request special services you can provide for them in your style or shop.

You want to pick a special feature or a customization of service that only your shop provides. Especially locally or within driving distance of other tattoo shops in your radius. Start your customization and special feature promo online, too using Facebook and Instagram flyers. Start Facebook tattoo groups to connect with community to new custom elements and special features to gain awareness and more clientele.

Let's start off with some constructive brainstorming for ideas of special features of service you can offer and customization. Feel free to get a pen and paper and write down all the features that click into your head during this brainstorm exercise. Draw a line in the middle of the pater. Then you write decent special feature on the left-hand column. Next, write great special feature/ customization on the right-hand side of the paper. Create your own ideal customization experience, whatever first pops up. Try to write 10 things down on each side of the paper in 5 minutes to get your mind into an alpha wave peak flow. You cannot formulate ideas better on a beta brainwave stage. A quick hack to do is think of an idea and subject matter, then pace, or take a walk. Yes, by walking on it, your brain neurons start to electrify and connecting to help you problem solve and think more efficiently and transparent.

Therefore, under decent special features, I would write down glow-in-the-dark tattoos and cover-up tattoos, to give you a few ideas. Then, once you have those two ideas locked into your thought bubble, you further build on them little by little. You can build daily or throughout the day and by the end of the week, you can have a thorough and new innovative concept or possibly a whole business plan. Who knows? It's totally up to how your mind works or how you work your mind.

Next, column under great special feature slash customization, you can write down body piercing, implants, and dermal piercing. Then build on this, too, in your formulation of a thought bubble. This is just like the actual snowball effect. It keeps building up gradually bigger and bigger with momentum once it gets to rolling. Your mind is a computer and brilliant. You just have to write your own programs and give the orders and demand to produce desired thoughts and framework formulation. Remember, someone don't have to read the instructions if they know the direct instructions already. Anything is possible and you can bend the laws of the universe if you so will. All you have to do believe, desire, and work to achieve.

Keep trying to get your desired creative results. You must keep pushing new ideas and new things. Don't be afraid to try and observe the marketplace, listen to the crowd and pay attention what your audience wants, needs, or dislikes. Use that to create a special feature niche.

Now let's get into the element added special feature and customization of offering body piercing at your shop or with your mobile tattoo services provided. First you need to know how to do body piercing and the different type of piercing to offer. Or you also can hire a trained expert body piercer. To learn how to body pierce, you can go into body piercing shops to see if they can train you, do an apprenticeship thru them or simply tag along. You can also watch body piercing training online.

You may need to take a safety and sanitation course or get registered as a certified body piercer at your county Board of Health Department. Maybe a first aid course, too. Again, do all your research first and local homework. When doing body piercing, they have a body piercing kit with a black canvas bag full of all your body piercing instruments, like to pierce your tongue, fixtures and utensils including different piercing needles. You need to make sure your sterilization and sanitation is all in check with the proper practices and cleaning chemicals. Also all biohazard and disposable material, too.

They have body piercing starter kits online or at tattoo and body piercing supply chain ranging from $90 to $200 typically. There are more advanced and costly body piercer kits or instruments. It's also different body piercing available to offer as a special feature and customization like doing dermal piercing or known as implants, which is a new trend that a lot of celebs and people doing. Especially with the ladies. Some dermal implants are studs or diamonds. These can screw on and off the skin once it's planted in the skin. It's an under-the-skin approach. They enable it to be implanted in different parts of your body canvas. It's not like through and through spots like the ear, lip, or tongue. It's essential that you are trained correctly to do a proper job offering this special feature. Even your hired shop body piercer, too. You don't want to find a backyard body piercer that is winging it and don't know what they are doing fully or in case of an emergency. Like if you do not center the tongue correctly, you can hit a main vein and paralyze the tongue or have them bleeding out in a catastrophe. Get educated on all ways and take your time. Do not rush into this craft just to offer a special feature to generate more shop cash flow. You must do what you can maintain and acquire full knowledge or expertise in.

When I ran a two-in-one practice with a tattoo shop and a body piercing shop, I took all the body piercing how-to courses and the safety courses. I still did not pierce, even though I knew how. I hired two women to do all the body piercing. One full-time and the other part-time. A woman body piercer fits my shop best because I learnt thru experience that other females like when women pierced them. Especially in those private part areas. They simply did not feel comfortable with a guy touching them. When the guy came to help them, the majority of the woman clients would decline or walk out and never return. Once I lost out on earned revenue, I saw clearly I had to adjust and change staff and being an early adopter by observing the customers, their demands and suggestive language. It took me months to learn because I dove in head-first, thinking I was going to totally crush it off the rip and kill my nearest competition. Therefore, I can share this story with you to save you a costly mistake. You can hire a guy body piercer. However, make sure you have a lady body piercer, too, and you won't miss out on providing your special features as advertised and promised. Whereas, it takes time to progress. Some low percentage actually gets a direct hit or lucky with exponential customization growth.

Body piercing is optional and may not be your speed or cup of tea even though it goes hand-in-hand with tattoo audience. Let's say you went with doing a special feature providing your glow-in-the-dark custom tattoos. You would provide a variety pack of glow-in-the-dark tattoo options at a deal to add value at a better rate than the competitors. You can go online and find glow-in-the-dark ink, black-light ink, or transparent ink. I would order my glow-in-the-dark ink from China or the UK for the different glow-in-the-dark colors. You may find some at your local tattoo chain supplies. All my foreign-imported glow-in-the-dark ink was a better quality ink versus the domesticated ones.

Now with doing customers' custom glow-in-the-dark ink tatts, you have got to be very careful and observant. You cannot see it clear once you wipe it or the ink, period, because it's transparent mostly. You need to rely on your prior tattoo experience, like I told you about in the first chapter of Tattoo 101. Making it systematic until it's automatic by tracing your patterns over your stencil prior to tatting, hitting all your lines and strokes to attack those angles and pain points of the tattoo with confidence. Well, with glow-in-the-dark tatting, you cannot have room for error. Unless you tatting in a dark room or under a black-light lamp. It's different methods and ways to skin a cat, but you need to be confident in your skillset either way. This is another custom feature that you would think is a piece of sweet cake until you make a huge mistake. It's basically like tatting blind with confidence, hitting and knowing all your hard lines and shading areas, too. You cannot rely on following the blood spurts/beads on the stencil layout over your canvas. Because you can tatt areas where people do not even bleed after shading or a simple line. Remember, you cannot have your regular tattoos with consistency and your glow-in-the-dark custom special feature tatts inconsistent with huge hiccups. You don't want your client to get laughed at in the dark, at home, or out on the town at night because they will point the finger back at the tattoo artist and shop. Therefore, you risk bad reviews with your whole custom feature of glow-in-the-dark tatting. Remember, with bad shop reviews word spreads fast, and you will not make a profit off your special features, period.

Customizations customers are always right. Don't force them to do it just because it's your new special feature or offer and it is an easier job for you, the same model most shops making quick money does. Customizations can also be in subject and style of tatting. Like simply, wild, color, animate, or black and grey. Artistry is also customization where you display your art form and custom style, too. Just like in the same fashion of developing your style.

You can also add feature in the shop like your own brand and tattoo logo merchandise of shirts, lady tees, hats, masks, wristbands, hoodies, stickers, glow sticks. Also tattoo supplies like ink, gloves, needles, or tattoo guns for sale. You can have special feature where you fix or design custom tattoo guns.

If you have an icon or special features out front of your shop like awnings, umbrellas, parked limos or mascot, you can brand it with your customization to promote outside your shop. Or even if you have a mobile tattoo van parked out front in the shop parking lot, you can also promote awareness and market your special features and customizations.

Lastly, remember if you choose to watch tutorials online on how to do body pierce techniques or how to do the best glow-in-the-dark tattoos effectively, that you still need the hands-on experience before you can get paid for your special features and custom services.

You can definitely use tattoo cover-ups for your special features just like that reality tattoo show *Tatt Nightmares*, where they specialize in cover-ups only and owned that space dominate.

- Chapter 9 -

"Shop Management"

Shop management is the heartbeat to having a great-running shop and a successful practical environment. From safety, accountability, to time management. Theft prevention and influential leadership skills are all required to maintain a thriving shop and cultivate a healthy tattoo culture workplace. Regardless if you have a small shop with a few employees or a shop on the busiest strip in your city with a dozen employees, you need to treat it like you running a top executive Fortune 500 company like Amazon. Take it serious and always be professional, because it's still a business, big or small.

Then you need to get you the right acquired help. You want to hire someone full-time to meet all your standards of operations, ethics, culture, and brand style. It's your business. Therefore, you have to lay out all your visions, goals, and company expectation with development. You want someone to be all in and devoted to the cause to perpetuate the tattoo shop experience.

You can be unfulfilled if you put your energy into training people who are not present or take ownership or observant with responsibility. You need them to be able to connect with people, staff and customers. They have to be equipped with people skills and customer service experience. You can hire people that are smarter than you or better than you at that job of management to work for you. Their engagement and commitment to make progress and connections. You don't need a person policing your environment or staff micromanaging everything, every second. You can hire security guards for all that. You want someone with accountability skills with love, no sugar-coating, and that you can depend on to make the corrective executive management decisions necessary to the shop's best interest at heart. Release any relationships that don't work. You need to look for shop managers that will make an impact and willingness to stay late and put in the extra work it takes to sustain a thriving work environment and tattoo culture in service. They need to be able to say No! A true leadership manager knows how to say No and tell staff No! For instance, I had a tatt artist that would keep asking to go on break by leaving the shop to go home real quick, despite all her downtime regularly in the shop. I let her go on break to her house a few times, which she came back later and later with an excuse why her tardiness happened. I made a huge mistake by not saying No! I opened up a floodgate for her and other employees to walk all over me and take advantage because I did not lay down stern rules or say a simple No, displaying true management and leadership skills.

A true leader and manager must possess these traits, skills, and regulation principles. Most of all, how to truly manage. Management is defined as the act or art of managing, control, or judicious use of means to accomplish an end. Also can be the group of those who manage or direct an enterprise.

The main quality is they need to be able to manage a team and have proof of prior experience. You can hire someone that only has the training from a management course without first hands-on experience and trust them with your shop business and brand if you like. Experience is always better and for them to be well-seasoned at what they doing. Accountability, organizer, risk management, and time management is all that need to be on their résumé or your checklist. Remember you don't just want to find a good shop manager, you want to get you a great shop manager who matches your shop principles and fits directly with your brand, too.

You need to have and establish a great relationship with your shop manager that consists of great communication, transparent, and trusty report. They need to be trusted with payroll and cash flow and accountable for the other artist relationship of transparency and delivery. They need to continuously push, lead, and manage the team with conveying message, mission, and teamwork ethics. To be a big engager and connector to create a company culture and great environment workplace and a welcoming space is all needed. It's all about curating an infinite leadership role, and finding people better than you with passion to do a better job with true experienced management skills.

Next you can start your search for the right match shop manager. You can use hiring apps, or go online to places that let you list jobs and all your qualifications and post an ad. Some sites even let potential employees bid for your job or interview. They allow people to compete and let you have your pick of the litter to your likeness. It's that simple. You schedule the ones you like for interviews and to come into the shop and meet the team. Don't rush this process of hiring. Take your time and let the right match and energy come into the shop naturally. Your team will gravitate towards your right shop manager and like them off the top. True leaders just have an undeniable presence and pay attention keen to little details.

Once you made a direct match, next you do a trial stage or a probation phase period. This is where you give the new-hire shop manager a test run on his management skillsets like leadership and work ethics. You can hire someone and think he or she is the right fit but lazy, or lack leadership skills it takes to manage the shop without you on a day-to-day basis. I fired two different shop managers for lying and accountability efforts. It was a great vibe and energy, both of them we clicked from the jumpstart we shook hands. However, they weren't proven yet. Then, surprisingly, a guy that used to come hang out at the shop daily, eating, laughing, and joking, I actually gave him a part-time job and he nailed it. Was one of the best shop managers ever. The team loved him, listened to him, and knew him. Whoever knew that this practical joker had a hidden jewel of a management skillset within him? Therefore, it's nothing wrong with giving people a chance or the right people a chance. You must still be adamant about testing them and their work ethic. I even wanted to hire that same practical joker shop manager to manage my food truck, too. That's how infectious his leadership skills were.

To test your new-hire managers, you put them under a few stress tests per week. A stress test is put them to work under pressure to see if they reflect, sink, or swim fast. Some even float or run and walk straight out. For example, I list all my shop managers know how to tattoo, just in case we get slammed pack busy. Then I stress test and have another shop artist's scheduled client coming in after he called into work on a sick absence or emergency. Then I'll sit back and see if the new manager did the tattoo work themselves or turned the client around dissatisfied and waste their time, transportation, and schedule on a promise by an artist at my business that's supposed to provide services rendered and delivered crispy. I would sit at the parking lot entrance and await to see if that one o'clock or two o'clock appointment is turnt around. Then I'd advise the new hire, then warn them once with a reprimand. The next time, I would make them pack up and fire them dead on the spot. If they don't have a business sense, they do not have longevity in my shop or building a brand and welcoming community culture.

The shop manager's focus cannot be split. You need to create a shop and brand vision for your shop manager together and execute, connect to it and build impact with the team to be better and extract value with clients and tattoo services. Your shop experience should be pleasing. It's hard to find best first hires. It's also harder to fire people, but you have to if you want to grow and succeed with your shop open for years. You need that drive and true voice in you to do what's right for you or your brand. Not being stuck on yourself and in thoughts and executed executively by taking best actions. Then stay present to achieve your goal and trust your heart and lead your business practice right the first time because you only get one start-up shop of all of you built with name, brand, and reputation on the line.

Therefore, please do not let nobody else or no bad seed planted management ruining your shop establishment you worked hard for and bust your ass with hard-earned cash and start-up capital. Remember there is not no tattoo rescues like bars. Once your tattoo shop crashes, it's going to burn up in smoke. Only way to revive that is change names, owners, and management branding. You need to reestablish trust and build new client experience, trust, and environment. And that is a whole new challenge nor easy. You have to prove yourself and buy creditability. You constantly have to prove it and perform. It's not just advertising and rebranding. Your shop management should be a dashboard of learning and leadership.

Next, is customer service, theft prevention and intervention. The shop manager must maintain order of shop, not just opening and close the shop, but being agile to shop theft and merchandise, to personal property or shop tattoo supplies. You can have a camera security system and monitor to allow people to see themselves. Also, you have to place signs inside to let people know it's cameras and they are being recorded. It does play a part in theft prevention. However, it does not stop people from theft. It can deter people. Your shop manager can also do some intervention so theft does not happen so easy. Like put things behind the casings, locking things up like your tattoo supplies and machines at your station drawers, and keeping the register shut. Also putting people getting tatted personal property up and putting the tattoo employees personal belongings in back-room lockers with combinations or padlocks, whatever you choose. This just a few of the many prevention and theft intervention methods your shop can adopt and model.

Shop maintenance is important and the shop manager's responsibility to maintain regularly. Even though you can hire additional staff or cleaning service crews to maintenance your shop after hours, too. From safety and sanitation with equipment, workstations, tattoo chairs, customer chairs, and the floors. It's all on you how you choose to do shop maintenance and lay down the ground rules for the shop manager and team. Remember accountability is essential in maintenance, making sure each artist cleans, sterilizes, and disinfects before and after.

Lastly, maintenance tip and followed practice of prevention post-pandemic is using COVID-19 chemicals and cleaning before shop open and maintaining a safe, sanitary, and structural environment. Display leadership skills to shop management and follow all the CDC recommended guidelines with COVID-19 preventions from masks, wash hands, to cleaning chemicals and utensils. Like a UV COVID light to clean and disinfect, keeping people safe.

- Chapter 10 -

"Franchising"

Finally, in this last chapter, we will tackle making your shop plural, meaning in multiples. This is an added bonus trade of franchising. This is only an option once your shop has been a total success all around with your reviews, fan base, brand, style, tattoo culture you created, ultimate tattoo experience, and finally a great team and tattoo blueprint to follow. Mainly your clientele is booming and standing around in lines that wrap around the corner of the shop when you fully booked up with clients for 3 weeks to a full month just to get a 45-minute small tattoo session at your shop or with you personally. The point of franchising is to scale and expand your tatt brand. The revenue stream and cash flow is appreciated and it comes with inevitable growth and great structural systems in process to cultivate success at its best.

Some people do franchise strictly to monetize their business. It is nothing wrong with wanting to franchise solely for money purposes. However, you should do it out of adding value to your business and people's lives by being a service to people. That way the ultimate service and tattoo experience impacts people, which outweighs more than any money or tangibles, because it's priceless. Those memories, symbolism you provide to be getting your tattoo services is meaningful to most clients and impact them more than you know. Especially if it's a tattoo of a loved one or any artwork from a loved one that passed or alive. I have done Rest In Peace tattoos, portraits, signatures, even baby footprints, all of people's cherished moments and loved ones, which all means a lot, usually leaving clients emotional, which creates a lasting imprint and memory. Then you created an everlasting first-time shop impression touching each individually. Therefore, sometimes when money is the motive or main interest, you can be trapped by greed and blinded by the dangled carrot of delusion. Sometimes when you aim big, you also lose big. It's always risk and reward factors in any business or franchise and corporate organizations. All go thru the same operational and scalable profit risk and reward.

The odds are against you pursuing a successful profitable business. Over 85 percent of the start-up businesses fail within the first 5 years and file bankruptcy bailout. You must look very deep before you leap. Do your homework and all thorough research first and don't rush. Take your time. Remember success comes in steps.

Now let's break down franchising—the meaning, differences, dos and don'ts for your starting off successful franchise branching out. Franchising is a joint venture of your brand and business with others that can buy in and invest with you for franchisee fees, own locations, supplies, and branding same practice and equity. People are paying to join.

A franchise is a right or license granted to an individual or group. Also a constitutional or statutory right or privilege. A franchisee is one granted a franchise. A franchiser is a franchisee or franchisor. If you hear or use any of these terms, you have to know the true definitions and the difference dealing with franchising.

You must remember your core metrics and reality of what you want to do with your shop and brand. You need to understand the mechanics of what you want to do before actual franchising as an option. Like if your whole shop goal is just to have multiple shops in your town locally or possibly other big cities, then you do not need to franchise and have franchisees to join your venture of tattoo brand. You need to remain the sole owner or co-owner if you already have initial additional start-up partners with your tattoo business. You just have to reframe your budget and the conceptional amount of experience it will take to maintain a successful tattoo practice and duplicate or kindle that same tattoo environment in a new place and location while keeping your fingers crossed for best results versus a flop of a nightmare. Therefore, franchising is not for you if you merely want to own multiple shops in different areas that you run hands-on exclusively.

When franchising you do not have to have an IPO (initial public offering) in the stock market like a lot of household-name franchises do. You do not have to be worried or intimidated about trying to compete with the big franchiser companies and brands. Nor do you have to worry about pressure attempting to be the tattoo business franchise to hit the stock market with shareholders and public stock for people to buy and invest in. The realization of microfranchising need not to have no stress and it can be as big or exclusive as you see fit long as it works for you, your brand, and franchisors with success. Confidence and competence is all you need to achieve in franchising. Take the fight to them.

How to franchise: First step is offering your franchise shop open, finding franchisees in your community or other cities, giving them your franchise package deal. You need to draft franchisee agreements and contracts stipulated to all your prerequisite, including start-up fees. You have to include the time stipulation you want to license your tattoo business brand for. Just like the lease at your tattoo shop space, it could be yearly, 2 to 5 years, or 6 months at a time. It's whatever options suit you and your co-founders best to franchise additional shop exclusive rights.

Next is location and area, it has to be a just location within your approval and city and state zoning permits. The franchisee needs to have the building they own or leasing to have all standard working function. Windows, bathrooms, fire detectors, working sinks, and proper electrical outlets. You need to have it inspected for safety standards. Also, do a walkthrough, too.

Then you do a written deposit you want for licensing your franchise to the franchisee. This is usually a fee upon signing the franchise agreement. Fees vary in start-up franchises. You set your own with your correct prior company and brand valuation, then divide that by a 15 or 20 percent ratio. You can even do a 10 percent franchise fee. It's totally up to you. However, make sure your franchise valuation start-up fee for all potential franchisees that want to be a part of the great team, brand, and tattoo community have a fair and reasonable valuation. Don't pass Go with nothing outlandish and not a proven valuation, too farfetched to where you scare off potential franchisees with a hefty deposit. You do not want people thinking you are running a get-rich-quick scheme or sticking to your tattoo practice, brand, and implementations to follow the steps and franchising as a fraud. Remember throughout this book reputation is everything and you will be known for something. Therefore, what do you want your reputation to be? You must always think first and don't pick up bad habits. Drop them and develop good and great habits to practice. Then your rep will be known as great with all good things attached to it, including work ethic, trust, and delivery. Not a bad rep for being untrustworthy, undeliverable, and a shady person or practice.

Now I am going to give you some quick framework to do a realistic correct tattoo franchise valuation. Remember, a company valuation is a projection based on past proven cash flow or sales, and data, too. It's the estimated or determined market value of a thing. Or also the act or process of valuing, especially the appraisal of property. Whereas, value is a fair return or equivalent in money, goods, or services for something exchanged. The monetary worth of a thing. Also relative worth, utility, or importance.

Let's say if for example your tattoo shop and brand sales per year is $250k, you doing a 10 percent valuation, then you would have the franchisees put down a start-up franchise fee of $25k. It's that simple framework and you can do the same percent off your estimated valuation by 15 or 20 percent, whatever you choose. Again, just be careful not to be too greedy and running the franchisee off.

How to find franchisees? Tap into tattoo groups and community all over. Promote your franchise brand package and services you looking for artists or business owners to come be a part of franchise. You can recruit people around town and pitch to them or you can use online promo and ads. Or you simply can do franchise awareness on your social media platforms. Remember your social media presence power that you learnt from previous branding chapter. Your social media presence is pivotal to promotion and your franchising push. Use that same social media framework you learnt in previous chapters, too, and model it to your franchise drive. Model it into your franchising. Again, all of this ciphers and go hand-to-hand.

You can do virtual tours or videos of your shop brand equity and successful operations like a playlist. Give them a public display A thru Z in your franchise package tour and all proven concepts and factual data results. They may want to see your proof of sales, service, and all additional revenue streams, including from social media branding and ad revenues with sponsorships for the past year or 5 years. All tangible incomes and spreadsheets. If your past earned income does not match or check when the franchisee or their financial advisor asks to see the numbers you have to provide, or else they will slide and wave bye fast. Always be clairvoyant and capitalize on all opportunities. Sometime in this space, you may only have or get one opportunity to close or make an impression and leave a great impact.

You can also go online and draft contracts templates to follow and fill in the blank. Including franchise template drafts where you stipulate A, B, C and what you need, then X, Y, Z what you expect and require from them in the franchise agreement contract. Whatever you like, just remember not too complex. Simplify cut and dry to the point. You don't need a big long social media outlet user agreement dire language extensively.

Finally, you can franchise your brand exclusively. It does not have to be your tattoo shop business plan, operations, and scope. You can do exclusive minor franchise packages and agreement for brand use only. You can license someone to use your brand name, theme, and style developed. I've even permitted people, companies, and other brands to use my brand name with being compensated in exchange for licensing. Brand integrating or franchise integrating is all doable, possible, and profitable.

When you take action and do your thorough franchising probing and take your time to formulate a great franchise plan to present a decent and fair proposal to sign a joint venture with to a beautiful established partnership.

Thanks for reading, educating yourself *How to Tattoo and Start-Up Business* or listening to Audible. Leaving you a bonus!

Bonus Page

Now that you done completed the *How to Tattoo and Start-Up Business*, I would like to leave you with a book bonus. This is a DIY (do-it-yourself) added bonus tip of how to make a homemade tattoo gun, needle, and ink. This is a way to extract value from nothing or little to no means or resources. You can make a homemade single-needle tattoo gun with all household items. You don't need no money to do this unless you do not have some of the household items I name and mention to follow.

This how to make a homemade tattoo gun from scratch is a fun experience and easy steps to duplicate to get your finish goal of a complete operational tattoo gun out of nothing without spending money. It also allows you to make multiple homemade tatt guns or when needed under any circumstances, including homemade ink too from scratch.

It's also an old jailhouse style machine. I would have people request and demand these homemade tatt guns because they liked the single needles and prison style tatting like that black and grey look with that old India ink. People have paid me $500 per homemade or jailhouse tattoo gun alone. People would come into my shop and ask for them even as collectible tattoo items to put on display at their shop or tattoo expos. You will not get this bonus or framework how to build a homemade tattoo gun, needle, and ink from scratch with simply household items only nowhere else or online. I took the time out to handwrite this book and bonus tip to give y'all value no matter what. Especially if you have a love for tatting, tattoos, and the tattoo community culture. You can leave me pics, tag me, or email me your finished results of your homemade gun you learnt to put together with this bonus tip. Also share the pics with me if you actually did tattoos with clients, friends, or family using your homemade machines.

The first step is to get a clear Bic ink pen. You should be able to find this type pen around the house, in cabinet drawers or desktop shelves. If you cannot find a Bic ink pen or don't have one, you can go to the dollar store and get a pack of Bic pens for 99 cents. Again, make sure it's a clear Bic ink pen. Although, nowadays many people don't use regular ink pens or handwrite because of their e-devices and being tech savvy, especially with Millennials and Gen Z's.

Now once you have located and obtained a clear Bic ink pen, you need to strip it down and out. This will be your barrel and whole homemade tattoo gun. Keep the black pen cap, too, because that is what you are going to need to sit the small motor on to. Get you a razor and slice/saw off half of the black pen cap first. Not too much or too less because the black pen cap is for your whole ink barrel to go inside of. It has to be able to fit and go through both sides of the cut-off pen cap. Next step, you bend with your finger that black pen cap pointer tip into an L-shape. Meaning bend it down until it's vertical. Not too far down or barely bent. It should look like an L-shape upside down. Then place the whole Bic pen inside to make sure it fits still and goes thru the half-cut pen cap with its bent arm tip.

The next step is pulling the pen filler out of the Bic pen. Pull it out from the bottom of the pen tip and it should come straight out. You should have an empty clear Bic pen barrel. Find some dental floss string or regular thin string from loose fabrics around the house. You double-wrap the string and saw back and forth until it cuts thru the plastic Bic pen. You want to saw fast to create friction to cut thru the plastic precisely. Now you only cut half of the Bic pen length. You keep the bottom end that the ink filler and pen tip goes into. You can toss the top half of the rest of the Bic pen in the trash. Then place that part of the tip bottom of the other half of the Bic pen barrel into that half-cut pen cap.

Get you a pair of fingernail clippers to pinch the ink pen head tip where the ink comes out of. Be careful not to clip the actual V-shape hole off the pen head that the small tip fits into. It's a little gold brass-looking tip. You will tell if you pulled it off correctly because it'll have ink all over the back end. Also you can see the hole in the head of the pen where the rest of the ink comes down thru.

The next step is to pull the pen filler apart with a napkin to get the ink out of it. You keep the pen head that little brownish brass V-shape pointer. You can fan the pen filler to shift gravity to get the filler ink out or submerge in warm water, then blow on the back end to give it a little boost to flow out. Next, make sure you clean all the ink out the pen filler thoroughly. You don't want to get that into someone's skin and risk infections. Use a small sheet of toilet paper. Tear off one square and twisted small and long, preferably diagonal. Damp the tissue and insert it into the empty pen filler to get the remaining ink spots until it's see-through. Twist the damped tissue until the whole pen filler is transparent. You can keep doing this with however many pieces it takes to clean it.

After your pen filler is cleaned out, get that razor and slice the pen filler in half. Keep one half to place back into the pen head snuggle after you cleaned the pen head out with tissue in the same manner to get the ink left over out. Then place that into the shell of your Bic pen barrel with the pen cap still attached. With the other half of the pen filler, cut that into 3 pieces. One of the 3 small empty pen filler pieces will be used as the wheel to the motor that spins your machine around and needle up and down. Keep the other 2 pen filler small pieces for extras. Don't throw them away. They will come in handy.

Now it's time to make the homemade needle. You can use the spring out of a hairspray bottle or even the spring out of a Bic lighter. Break them open until the spring pops out, get 2 fingernail clippers to grasp each end of the string and heat it up over the stove or use another lighter. Have someone hold the flame over the coiled-up spring until it turns red hot, then pull both ends with the nail clippers slowly apart and watch the spring straighten out. Do this process over until it's straight. Measure the stretched-out spring to the half-barrel Bic pen that's attached to the black pen cap and add an extra half-inch to leave room to attach the needle to the tattoo motor. Then clip it with the nail clipper with that exact measurement. It's okay to clip off extra versus too short to fit. With extras, you can always clip and trim a little off as needed.

The next step with your needle is to sharpen by getting sandpaper a fair grade, not too rough or too smooth. Place the tip of the spring at an angle under your index finger to sand it to a point. The tip of your spring needle should make a V-shape, not slant knife shape. You don't want to scar nobody or cut nobody open. Put the needle up into the light to see the tip sharpened progress until it's just right. Be patient and take your time. You should be able to press your thumb down on the needle lightly and if it sticks into your thumb without pricking your thumb with blood. However, if your needle drops and don't stick to your thumb, it's too dull and needs to be sharpened more. Another quick hack to sharpen is place the sandpaper on the motor running the homemade gun to spin the paper around on the wheel while placing the needle on it to sharpen easier all around. Disinfect the needles and you can burn them with a quick flame before you sharpen, too.

The last part before we make the ink is to get a motor. The challenge is looking for an old CD player or cassette players that has those little battery-ran motors. If you don't have one at home, you can go to a Radio Shack-type store to find one. Break the CD player apart to get the motor out. Make sure you don't pull the two black and red wires coming out of the motor. You need the two negative and positive wires attached to the motor to enable your machine to work and you attach them to your battery pack.

You attach the small CD player or tape set motor to the black pen cap tip that you bent earlier vertical, to place it on and Saran Wrap it down tightly. Wrap a finger-size Saran Wrap piece around the outside circle grey motor to the pen cap tip to where it's attached firmly. You shouldn't be able to move it, period.

Then you get the plastic pen filler cut extra piece to place it onto the motor spinning round piece sticking out. This is to make a wheel to attach the needle to. Now you can place the plastic pen filler piece straight onto the motor head circle piece directly, or you can turn it sideways and poke a hole in it to fit around the motor. If you turn it sideways and poke a hole to fit on the motor spinning wheel, it's easier to poke another small hole for the needle to fit. Next, you can bend the needle into an L-shape vertical at the top part of the needle into that plastic wheel pen filler small piece. This is what makes your needle spin and causes it to go up and down in the attached pen barrel. Or you can choose the other option of putting the pen filler piece directly on the motor wheel and melt down a small piece of that extra spring no more than a quarter or half-inch. Then melt a piece of pen filler to your needle top piece without bending it, instead put a small hole in the plastic pen filler piece attached to your top part of the needle after you melt it down on it. Then the motor spinning wheel with plastic and spring sticking out will go into the plastic hole top part attached to your needle to make it go up and down and spin to tatt. Either method works.

Finally, it's time to make your battery pack to start your machine up. First, you get a four-pack of AA batteries. I use 3 batteries, 2 new ones and one used battery to get my homemade tattoo gun just the right speed, or you can use all used AA batteries in your battery juice pack to slow the machine down to the speed you like, especially for shading areas.

A portable battery back allows you to be mobile with using batteries only. No foot pedals or electricity and outlets used or needed. Therefore, that's a huge plus and advantage because you can take that homemade gun anywhere, including tatting outdoors.

Next, find some sturdy paper around the house like construction paper or even a manila envelope and a file folder as paper. You place all 3 AA batteries on top of each other forming one row and roll the paper up over the batteries until it's covered tightly. Next, roll the batteries up slowly and firmly 3 times around with paper, then cut the rest of the paper off that's extra. Tape the rolled-up batteries in the paper up. The paper is used as a shell and wrap to the batteries to keep them intact, also to make direct contact just like if they were still in a CD or cassette player to power it up. It's the same concept. Instead of powering up your mobile battery-powered device, you are powering your tattoo homemade gun to operate with that same old motor. You also can easily replace the old batteries easy by pushing the new ones in from the bottom. The batteries will come out of the top.

The last step is wiring from the black and red negative/positive two wires running out of the machine/motor. Find speaker wire or gauge wire to attach and twist them separate on both wires to connect to each negative and positive wires, then wrap them with a little electrical tape so they don't touch, period. Each speaker wire you use or piece of wire should be an arm length to attach to your battery pack and have wiggle room to move around freely. You connect the positive wire to the top part of the AA battery head and tape it down. It should be the red wire, but some motors may not have different colors wires or colors at all. All you have to do before tapping the wires down to both ends of the battery pack is a test run. You place one wire on top and the other on the bottom, and if that motor wheel starts spinning, then your negative and positives is correct. If it don't budge, it's wrong and you have to switch the wires around. After you see it jump, move, or spin, place electrical tape or Scotch tape down firmly, making contact. The negative or black wire runs to the bottom of the battery pack. And there you have it. Your first homemade tattoo gun project.

Let's go back over the steps in order simplified and fast track.

First step, get you a Bic clear pen, cut the pen and pen cap both in half. After, you take the pen inside filler out. Use a piece of string like dental floss to saw off pen barrel and a razor for the pen cap barrel. Then bend the pen cap tip in an L-shape down vertical to fit your motor on. Get fingernail clippers to pull the tip of pen head off and clean with tissue all the ink out of the pen filler tube. Cut the pen filler in half and then the half into two additional half pieces for your wheel to your motor attachment.

Next step is get a spring from a lighter or spray bottle, straighten it with pulling it apart slowly by nail clippers, a heat flame so it can straighten easy from the coil stage. Get sandpaper medium grade to sharpen needle to a V-shape point, not a slant angle knife shape to cut or scar someone. Do the thumb trick to test your needle to see if it sticks to your thumb without falling out to see if it's sharpened right.

Then, find an old CD player or cassette player and strip the little motor out of the back of it with the 2 negative and positive wires attached. Place the motor on top of the bent pen cap and wrap it around tightly with a small piece of Saran Wrap. Place a piece of pen filler to the motor spinning knob to attach a wheel to make your needle move. Place pen barrel into the half of pen cap and align the needle straight into the barrel and bend the top part into the place wheel attached to the spinning motor.

Final step is making the battery pack with 3 AA batteries rolled up into sturdy paper 3 times and wiring the wires from negative and positive off motor to the battery pack and taping them down to make direct contact. Tape it directly on battery prongs.

Now the last bonus is how to make homemade tattoo ink from scratch. Warning, please do not attempt to do this and burn up your home. Go outdoors. First step in burning your own ink is to find a jar of hair grease or chessboard pieces. These are items you can use to burn. The sole purpose is to catch the soot from the burnt grease or chess pieces. FYI, soot is a fine black powder consisting chiefly of carbon that's formed when something burns and that color's smoke.

Get you a file folder to perform a cone shape around the burning grease to catch all the smokey soot and scrape it off. Put your grease into a jar and make a wick to light the flame to burn the grease or chess pieces into the jar. All the soot should have a catcher lid on top of the file folder to scrape off afterwards, too.

Once you burnt the whole thing, it will be messy, you need to get a plastic spoon to scrape all the thick soot and place it into a can with a lid. Like an old shoe polish can, or a chewing tobacco can. Something with an airtight seal.

Next, mix it with a drop of shampoo till it's gooey. Get you an empty teardrop bottle and sterilize a small pebble rock or BB pellet to go inside the teardrop bottle with the ink to use as a shaker to mix the homemade every time before use. The soot you gather mixed with a little drop of shampoo or however many drops it takes to make that right concoction mix for ink results. Not too runny or too thick like clay, you will be able to judge it yourself to see if it's just right. This all was the prison-made way and style.

I hope you enjoyed and appreciate this value bonus of a homemade tatt gun and prison style!

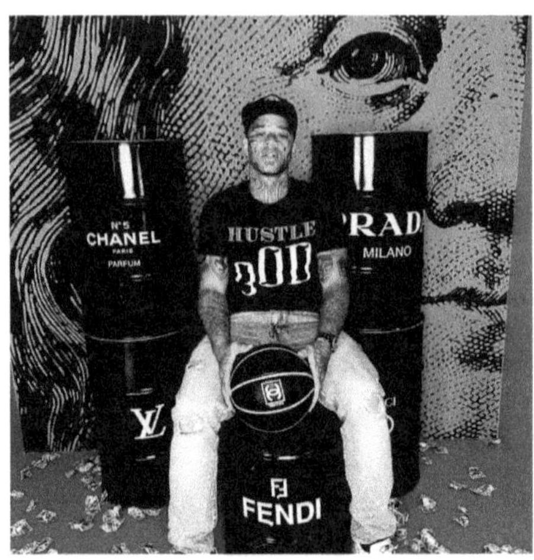

About Author

Hitachi Choparazzi is a New York City native, by way of Omaha, NE, who currently resides in Phoenix, AZ. Tattoo artist, shop owner, entrepreneur, turnt author.

He was the first Afro-American tattoo shop owner in Arizona. Ran the Chop Chop Tattoo Shop and Chop-A-Style Body Piercing 2-in-1 shop for years. Has over 17 years of tattoo experience. Learn how to tattoo from the inside being incarcerated for years and picking up a skillset with a passion and drive to be the best and deliver quality and consistency.

Hitachi Choparazzi started his own Chop-A-Style Publishing LLC company to help people incarcerated learn skillsets, personal development for their transition to help integrate back successfully into society. Also for entertainment with novels. Also his own library writing over 26 self-development and business development books and over 46 books and counting total. All from the inside.

Founder of Billion Dollar Blueprint movement and brand. Co-Founder of Incarcerated Lives Matter movement. Also Urban Bugatti shoes.

"This book is for y'all. I love to be of service, mentor, and educate y'all assist with skills and self-development. Love!"

Other Books and Scripts by the Author

Non-Fiction

- How to Rap; The Elementary Teaching of Hip-Hop

- How To Tattoo & Start-Up Business

- How To Digital Detox

- How To Start-Up a Food Truck Business

- How To Stop School and Mass Shootings: Dear Parents

- Incarcerated Lives Matter: The Hitachi Choparazzi Blueprint

- How to Love

- The Switch: A Social Awareness Self-Help

- Nipsey Hussle Lockdown Society Dedication–Tribute

- If Trayvon Martin Could Talk; Injustice

Fiction

- The Eagle and Weasel (1-5 series kids' book)

- She Go! (urban novel)

- Reality Show 3D-HD (urban novel)

- Hot Thots (urban novel)

- Liqz (urban novel)

- Paranormal Whisper (horror novel)

- Pimp of Da Ratchets (urban novel)

- Pimp of Da Ratchets II Vegas (urban novel)

- Pimp of Da Ratchets 3 Orange is Da New Pimp (urban novel)

- Hitachi (urban novel)

- Penitentiary Pimp (urban novel)

- Weasel Society (urban novel)

- The Big Pep and Plucker Story-She Go! Prequel (urban novel)

Screenplays/Scripts

- Top Notch

- Hot Thots

- Pimp of Da Ratchets

- Weasel Society

- Million Dollar Games–A Secret Society

- The Eagle and Weasel (animation)

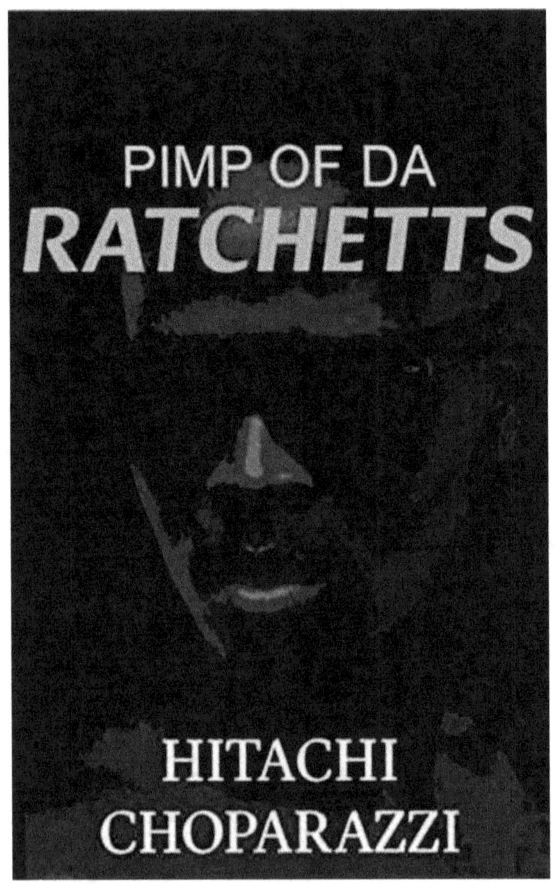

Available at Barnes and Noble and Amazon

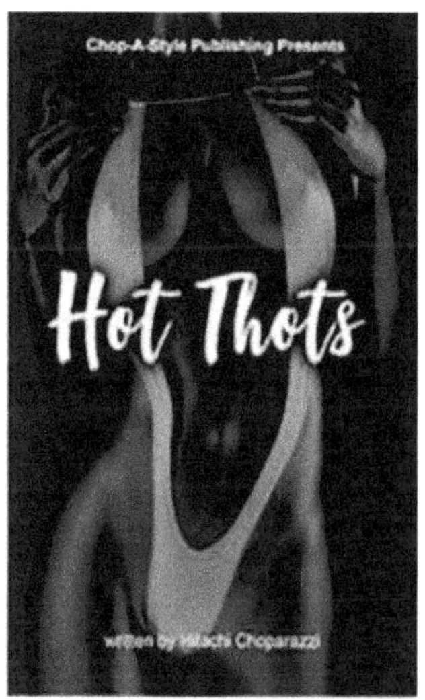

Welcome to the exclusive lives of 4 extremely hot THOTs. This book will show you how to spot a THOT. From THOT tops to THOT flops, all the way to THOT Snaps and claps.

This book is the first-ever with a double twisted love triangle. Watch as Chicago, LA, ATL, and Seattle THOTs entwine at Coachella.

Some on fleek and some looking cheap, but they all cheat! They all commit aTHOTery with their THOTery acts, shameless.

Raunchy, with steaming hot sex scenes to sex swings. From wild threesome ménages, and twerking, to bare-it-all raw. Too hot! THOT gum pop...

This page-turner is an eye-opener to the very end, with a bombshell-dropping, shocking ending. The secret life of THOTs

Available at Barnes and Noble and Amazon

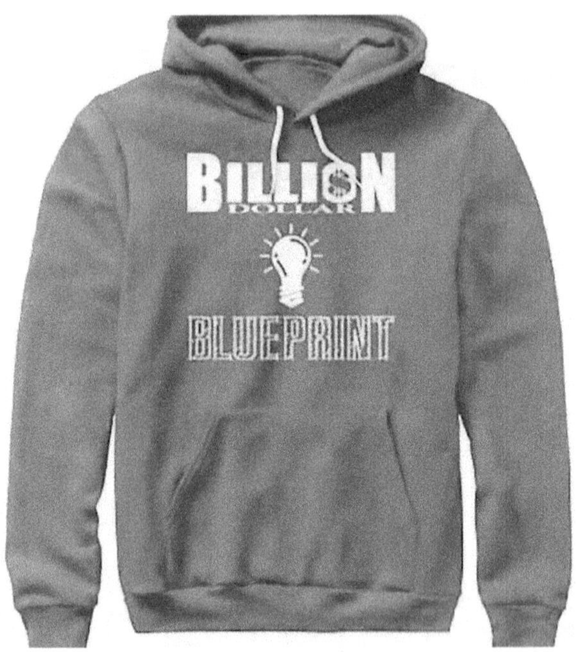

Billion Dollar Blueprint is a movement we challenge and inspire you to find your individual blueprint. Our mantra is "We believe everyone has their own blueprint like everyone has their own thumbprint". With these three core principles

Education

Elevation

Innovation

Hitachi Choparazzi is the founder and CEO. Orders available to support incarcerated businesses.

Orders available at: billiondollarblueprintmerch.com